D0727852

Runaways

Elizabeth Swados

Introduction
by
Joseph Papp

BANTAM BOOKS
TORONTO NEW YORK LONDON

RL6, IL8+

RUNAWAYS

A Bantam Book / November 1979

The text for "Runaways" is written by Elizabeth Swados
except for the following contributions improvised
and formed by the actors:
HUBBELL—YOU DON'T UNDERSTAND—Bruce Hlibok
Spanish Argument From FOOTSTEPS—
Jossie De Guzman & Randy Ruiz
HUBBELL—OUT ON THE STREET—Bruce Hlibok
LAZAR'S HEROES—David Schechter
IN THE SLEEPING LINE—A. J.'s Dream—
Anthony Imperato; Roby's Dream—Venustra K. Robinson;
Jackie's Dream—Diane Lane; Lazar's Dream—
David Schechter; Eddie's Dream—Vincent Stewart;
Nightmares in Spanish—Jossie De Guzman,
Randy Ruiz, Ray Contreras.
English-Spanish translations by Jossie De Guzman

"Elizabeth Swados—A Runaway Talent" by Mel Gussow
appeared in The New York Times Magazine, March 5, 1978.
Copyright © 1978 by The New York Times Company.
Reprinted by permission.

Book design by Kenneth Kneitel

Photographs on pages 1–46 courtesy of Bill Schwab © 1978; on pages 57, 69, 72–73, 74, 88, 96, 123, 139, and 141 courtesy of George E. Joseph © 1978; and on pages ii–iii, 58, 60–61, 62, 65, 77, 80, 82, 85, 86, 90, 93, 95, 99, 100, 102, 105, 113, 114, 121, 125, 131, 134, 137, 143, 145, 148–49, 151, and 159 courtesy of Martha Swope © 1978.

ISBN 0-553-13390-X

Published simultaneously in the United States and Canada

Bantam Books are published by Bantam Books, Inc. Its trademark, consisting of the words "Bantam Books" and the portrayal of a bantam, is Registered in U.S. Patent and Trademark Office and in other countries. Marca Registrada. Bantam Books, Inc., 666 Fifth Avenue, New York, New York 10019.

PRINTED IN THE UNITED STATES OF AMERICA

0 1 2 3 4 5 6 7 8 9

Contents

Introduction
by Joseph Papp   vii

Prologue: Runaways in Rehearsal   1

Runaways   49

Elizabeth Swados—A Runaway Talent
by Mel Gussow   161

This book is dedicated to all the people
who taught me that theatre could be
much more than a business or a pastime,
and to all the people involved in
Runaways who proved that could be true.

Introduction

By Joseph Papp

RUNAWAYS is an unconventional musical. There is no obvious story line and none of the familiar theatrical devices which propel a musical work for the stage. It appears to be self-propelling and yet, to the close observer, there seems to be some invisible force at work in the musical-cries and word-spills pouring from the mouths of kids who have been hurt by life; some acute consciousness of a missing presence, from which the seemingly driverless vehicle is drawing its prime energy. The sensitive spectator is puzzled, even disturbed. "What is this specter haunting the play?" As an intelligent person he reasons: "This feeling of absence I am now experiencing must have to do with the fact that I am seeing all these young people together on the stage as though they were living under the same roof, so to speak, and yet, and yet....? The sensitive spectator is suddenly jolted with this realization: "There is no mother here looking after her brood! That's it! The mother is the missing person, obviously." But our sensitive spectator had read the program and recalled that RUNAWAYS was conceived as a perception of the world from a child's viewpoint and that parents were excluded from the play because they would only muck it up. "Why then," our friend asks, "do I have this sensation of absence, what is the mystery?" This question can be answered but only with a puzzle. Question: What is long, red, hairy, green, orange, baggy and plays a string instrument. Hint: a three-letter word, also a six-letter word, also a nine-letter word. Give up?

You guessed it. Liz, Swados, Elizabeth; mommy-daddy-teacher-truant officer-creator of RUNAWAYS . . . with long red hair, dressed in green and orange socks, a baggy pair of pants with a guitar. Liz, always at the center of the six month process of the making of RUNAWAYS, is the missing person on the stage. Elizabeth Swados, though she left that center a long time ago, is a constant presence in the work that grew out of her heart and mind. The sensitive spectator was wrong; there *is* a mother in the play and her name is Liz.

During the rehearsal period (the running of a household), she played other roles — teacher, judge, jury, plow horse, general, foot-soldier, slogging through the most difficult chores at the head of or in the ranks of her young charges. She nourished them and starved them. The rehearsal hall at times became a tribunal where she meted out punishment and reward with an even-handed justice.

Punishment took the form of fines and temporary withdrawal of affection; achievement was greeted with approval and child-like delight which would immediately dissipate all feelings of disapproval and rejection. There was a fine spirit of adventure in all the proceedings. Goals were set, attained, creating new and difficult objectives. Her face was as changeable as March weather — sometimes tense, lips white, jaws clenched, strumming her guitar with such vehemence as though the strings had been strung for piano. At other times her thin earnest face would light up with an incandescent smile of such radiance and complete innocence you could not distinguish her from one of the 11-year-olds in the company.

She plunged ahead with endless endurance, full of assurance and then overwhelmed by vulnerability. Snappy, bright eyed, tough, inspirational, she led her troops into new discoveries of themselves, pushing them beyond their limits, and herself beyond hers. The fact remains that she was a perfectionist and demanded much more from herself than from her cast and musicians. She created a home for her runaways and she ran it with a firm but loving hand. Out of her own body came the nourishment which fed the young flock and brought the show into being. The shaping of the show therefore was as much the shaping of young lives. With no preconceived technique of communications, all evolved in the day-to-day process of making the play work.

It was a remarkable affair, a unique lesson in human relations as we watched the kids grow. There were times when Liz was their tormentor and also their last hope. And there were times when as she was herself tormented and they, her last hope. Through the interaction of each individual in the production with Elizabeth, there emerged a highly personalized character finding its true expression on the stage. Here life and art were so intermingled that the differences were barely distinguishable. The exploration taking place touched at the very heart of the learning experience — direction, purpose, goals, discipline and love. The nature of this experience and its effects lie deeply buried in the written and performed work. But from time to time it makes its way to the surface and then we have our sensitive spectator rubbing his eyes, for he has imagined that he has seen the ghostly outline of a thin, red-haired young woman with a barely visible halo around her head, standing center stage and smiling.

Prologue

Runaways in Rehearsal

If you decide to make a play
    about Runaways
don't just go to the ghettos of
    your city
don't just look at the kid whose
    parents beat him up
don't expect, even, that Runaways
    are only kids.
Look everywhere, in the eyes of everyone.
Start with yourself.
The world is full of people running.
You are a world full of questions.

When we made *Runaways*
we spent hours and days
running in place
as fast as we could
our thighs, our calves
our knees screaming.
We were sweating, our
hearts were pounding
we tried to find the sensation
of urgency
of *having* to leave.
We all wanted to erase different nightmares.
But we *all* had nightmares.

Things you run from:

parents

ugh

police

hatred

dope

fear

nightmare

growing up

problems

responsibility

dying

no understanding

ourselves

anxiety

trouble

smelly garbage

bad food

city

teachers

bad homes

the strap

drugs

whiskey

girls on 145th St.

truth

fire

love

bad friends

selfish people

violence

my father's shoe

images

bad memories

constructive criticism

very good friends

funny people

foxy girls

phone calls from Mother

my loving brother

Pamona Junior H.S.

embarrassing situations

cars

drag queens

too much fun and games

the old gang

perverts

caring grandmothers

gym

bad vibes

phoniness

pocket-happy bitches

street gangs

lies

honesty

Conjure the sound of a siren in your brain
the loud wail
its loneliness
the feeling of danger.
What is the siren inside of you?
Who would lock you up?
What are your prisons?
When you make a play about Runaways
you visit very dark rooms in your brain.

We discovered that fantasy saves us—
you can teach yourself to dream.
Out of a pile of paper towels
we made dolls, drums
even spaghetti and meatballs.
We made cousins out of empty shoes
boyfriends and girlfriends out of pillows.
Our parents became the elegant
photographs of antique furniture.
And we believed ourselves totally
as any loners would.

When you make a play about Runaways
you must consider that everyone is hopeful
looking for a family
whether it is a religious organization
a sports team, a street gang
a business office
or a theater group.
Everyone seems to need protection
some mapped-out answers
love
or what pretends to be love.
Or what pretends to be love.

Be careful.

Running away
from the binds of one family
can catch you in another.
The ropes may be different
but they're just as tight.

Repeating orders
over and over and over and over
in the army or a cult.
Being swept and courted
by a slick daddy
with a lot of drugs
cassettes, clothes and smooth words.

hild prostitutes and pimps
play a dangerous game of house—
getting addicted to a warm older body—
a kind of parent mix-up.

When you make a play about Runaways
be mistrustful of too much too soon.

Street rage has names:
riot loot rape gang
But what are the names
for the seemingly vacuum-cleaned
middle-class
tranquilized
loved-up, present-bought rages?
Years of proper behavior
good grades, high income
trying to live up to what
your parents were trying to
live up to before you—
builds ice over the spirit
builds a pressure in the house
unnameable and never admitted:
and a roof can crack and families break.

We learned that you don't
see those scars so easily.
But they are just as deadly.
Runaways *die.*
Don't ever forget. No matter what their
fathers did for a living. They *die.*

Litany

Drugs Drugs
the pressure of friends to be cool
the need to soften shouting voices
the need to brighten fading homes
Drugs—the need to laugh when
    nothing's funny
Drugs—the need to feel smart
the need to feel older
Drugs

Drugs
Watch out for the business of them.
Runaways get killed in drug traffic.
Watch out for the businessmen, the salesmen—
they don't wear ties.
If you do a show about Runaways
learn about the people who claim
to care about the spirit
but really want cash.
They are pushers.
They rank with the other following
Spirit Monsters:

Mothers that burn cigarette holes on their
   kids' shoulders
Mothers that beat kids black and blue
Drunken fathers that beat their kids
Relatives that beat their relatives' kids
Atom, hydrogen and neutron bombs
People who won't give you a chance to
   get straight 'cause they use you when
   you're on drugs
Rape
Fathers who beat their kids until they're
   dead
Mothers who trash-can their kids before
   they're two days old
Incest that ends up with the daughter
   pregnant
Incest that ends up with the son freaked
   out
Pimps who take children and sell them
   on the street

Our fantasies save us—
we draw posters against beating children
and dream of winning prizes.
We write secret songs
and play the lead in secret plays
and are adopted by secret
superfamous perfect people
and find a secret peace and
get secret vengeance on everyone
who laughed at us or ignored us.
If you make a play about Runaways
look for the good, bad and strange secret worlds.

If you're going to make a play about Runaways
learn fast that it's too easy
just to blame parents—
and boring.
The truth is like a torn-down
    building:
look down through floors and floors
    of history
the blown-apart rooms of your
    parents' own ideas
and the strange windows
where they look at you
and see themselves.
They had children before they'd
lived their own childhood out.

ometimes in an office
in a suit
dictating to a secretary
or talking on a phone
a father might
think of his bankbook
his wife his children
his car his house his
position his aging hairs
and graying muscles and snap
he might wake out of a
grown-up dream
asking what movie he's in.

Sometimes in a kitchen
a mother might juggle
four burners and four pots
consider her walk to
the grocery, her wish
to have a business, her
want to wear her
son's motorcycle jacket, her
longing to be a weight lifter,
she might look at the
wrinkles in her housedress
and the fading of her own eyes
and pop she'll wonder
what movie is this.

hen a man and woman
are unsatisfied
the vibrations get so strong between them
that they make—
sci-fi like—
a hologram:
an unhappy kid
a burning living being
called a Runaway
keeper of all unhappy parent vibrations.

Never underestimate
the gifts we are given to survive:
the secret drawers
the basketball courts
the graffiti walls
the guitars
the paints.
If you want to make a show about Runaways
look at the people who
put their lives into disco dancing.

atch a kid on a bicycle or skateboard.
Read what's on the sidewalks and the walls.
Watch who sells jewelry on the street.
These are songs of survival.
The best graffiti artists are Runaways.
They yell at the world with spray paint.
They put a big multicolored X
over what they think are lies.

Surviving is an art.
You need to be a genius
of the here and now.
If you want to know Runaways
you must be very quick
because they are magicians
between life and death.

There are all kinds of ways to con.
The street isn't the only market.
Imagine the enterprise of your dreams
and how you withstand
fear and loneliness.
Runaways have to fight off many voices.
The voices tell them they're going nowhere
bound to be nothing.
But secret voices tell them something else:
they are heroes.

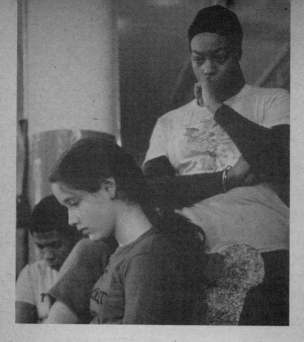

f you want to do a show about Runaways
realize early on
that the most frightening place to be
is always in between one place
and afraid of another.
Encourage all children
to demand their place on earth
but do not send them into the city alone.
They are rightful creatures
but they will get blown away.
Bam—

A story that frightens us:

A person started following me—he put
his hand in his pocket. I knew
he was following me so I put my
back against the wall.

We move into a new state, a new house
for the first time I am out playing
I come home the lights are out.
My mother is drunk she yells from nowhere
"What do you want?" and scares me.

I'm stoned and a man in a car is
chasing us trying to hit us. Can't
get away.

I'm bicycle riding they jump me for
my bike.

I fight with my sister
she throws knives through the door
she freaks out
I end up hugging her.

Hispanic voodoo ceremony
lady comes in chanting
takes off my shirt
takes white doves and they flap
their wings all over my body.

Walking home from school man
in skirt screams at me screaming.
He exposes himself
"You will go to the kingdom of
hell," he says.

If you want to make a show about Runaways
go visit real runaways.
They aren't superstars.
They aren't tap dancing in the ghettos.
Who are these kids
with spacey eyes
dull, bitter mouths?
They talk softly
or not at all.
They kill.
They get killed.

Their trust is a jewel—
it grows smaller and smaller.
You have to shout to
get through.

There's no real runaways
tap dancing on the streets.
They don't have the energy.

If you want to make a show about Runaways
don't underestimate
the power of material objects:
the heat or cold of a night
the thin or thick of a blanket
the dustiness of a road
the dark or light of a room
the wet or dry of weather
what the teachers are being paid
who got elected when who was assassinated
if they pick up the garbage
the men who go to the moon
how high a high rise goes
who cries at night
what the street sounds are.

We have made friends with toys.
We have talked to an electric bass.
We have told our skateboard
to take us crosstown.
Our boots have given us a new secret name.
We aren't crazy.
We're surviving.
If people won't hear us
we'll start with the *things* of the world.

If you want to make a show about Runaways
find a room.
Make its door the border of your country.
Pass through the door
and imagine the room's safety.
Protect its dignity.
Make the hours in that room one kind of life
no parents can intrude
disguised as lunch-bringers
no friends and gossip can intrude
disguised as relief
no Blues-Gonna-Blow-Everything-Apart can intrude
disguised as Personal Problems.

Imagine the room as a square
where the Never-Before-For-You could happen.
Make the hours in that room where you do more
    push-ups than ever before
where you discover new colors
where you play flutes with drumsticks
and sing through violins
where you shoot smack with bobby pins
and drive cardboard Rolls Royces
where you meet who you always wanted to be
those who wanted to be you.

This is what I do in my room:
I throw my knife into the wall.
I make up dances.
I read off an imaginary stock exchange
   ticker tape.
I make graffiti.
I play my guitar.
I have two pillows Simon and Sylvester
and I beat them and then apologize.
I do Kung Fu.
I do Karate.
I draw a special square in the
center of my room and sit there with
my most important thoughts.

*H*ide fear

If you do a show about Runaways
learn about
Hiding:

He's gonna kill me I'm gonna die oh no
please don't do anything I'm such a dummy
I'm gonna get chewed don't move I wish
you guys would cool out how am I gonna
get out of this you better not cry I can
become invisible I didn't mean it I can't
hold it I know he's gonna find me please
don't find me Jesus save me go away I
want to bash his head in don't touch me

the closet
the attic
under the bed
the roof with pigeons
the woods
men's room of a bar
in a tree
behind the boiler
on the canopy of the bed
in the bushes

Crazy

Who are the people who talk to the sky
the bums, stubble-bearded and
on the stoops.
You must've seen their fists
waving at the sky
their CB radio connections
to heaven
their arguments with imaginary friends.
If you want to do a show about Runaways
listen to them
but don't try to answer.

The old-time hoboes conversed
with the stars—
they made tin-can camps
and rubber-tire campfires.
They scraped stick-figure
symbol drawings in the mud
to warn other hoboes:
"cops nearby"
"trains near here"
"free food for simple work"
"danger."
If you want to make a show about Runaways
you must learn to make languages.

Learn the music of a crazy world:
Walk up to another person
say something positive
in a negative voice.
Say something negative
in a positive voice.
Strange
but you'll have heard it all before.

*T*he signals people give off:
He don't look anyone in the eyes.
She smiles too much.
It's like someone came and took everything
   out of her—she floats around like a
   balloon.
His quiet isn't just quiet y'know it's
   like before a gun goes off.
He screams so loud his veins start
   poppin like toasters but mad as he
   is it's a groove.
She has to be here first every day.
She's the last to leave.

Don't say nothin.
    Make like you don't notice she's around
        all the time.
    I will do everything I'm asked but
        keep my soul intact.
    He hasn't sat down since he got here
        he hasn't stopped talking. Don't let
        him go home alone.
    I never seen him mad and that makes
        me think he killed someone.
    I am out of my mind with exhaustion
        and it's excellent.
    He is terrifying and safe.
    Watch out for them nails in the floor—
        you could step on one and lose
        all your acting talent.

If you want to make a show about Runaways
learn to work together.
Watch a group of jazz musicians—
how their instruments
become mouths
how they talk to each other
like birds
in early morning work chatter.
They respect each other's
time to come in.
No one takes a solo too long
or plays out of balance with the others.
Listen: an explosion of sound.

There's a voice that can
sing a Runaways song
and it's not a famous rock and roll voice.
The voice
doesn't want to be famous (not yet).
It means what it says
or it wants to mean what it says.
It's a simple voice
like a single ray of sun
and it strikes the heart
like one finger touching one note
on a keyboard made of messages.

If you want to do a show about Runaways
listen for that voice.

V_ery original voices:_
a baby's first wail
the first time you learn any tune
two people fighting in another language
someone shrieking in fear
an incredible guffaw
people finding harmonies like a first kiss
an instrument and voice trying to talk
singing in the shower or in front of
   the mirror—fear free
bird calls and pigeon coos
a lullaby from a loving mother
a lullaby from a hating mother
a drunk's song
the song of someone in prison
the song of someone in pain
a surprise greeting
the mocking of a murderous gang
the songs without tunes inside the head
parents' voices behind closed doors
the imaginary song of making a mud castle
the work song that lays bricks and
   pulls ropes
the singer that rebels
the singer that quiets the mob
the voice that tames an animal
your own tune for conquering the universe

*R*unaways voices:
One black singer's voice is
as smoky as a good fog
over the dawn of our city.
Listen to her.
The Cuban dancer moves his
hips and holds the basketball
like a sacred rattle—he
tries to stare life into it:
New Jersey Voodoo.
Watch him.
Three young women
talk out the scat rhythm of
New Orleans to Harlem.
They juggle and punch each other
with giddiness
but they could kill.
They're hustling.

A wild punk jabbers off his
cosmic encyclopedic knowledge
his translation of the world into
Marvel Comic Sense.
He is laughing
but he could die.
A young man is deaf—
he hears vibrations and
the high pitch of sirens.
He learns to sing with his hands.
He is in incredible danger
in the noisy city
but he is surviving.

All these energies
all this sorrow
all this hopeful lethal vengeance
all this long dance and these songs
and the working of consonants
like machines clicking for perfection
all this fury
all this time of life where
the world lies and you work
to make it true, all this isolation
loneliness, worked on and loved
to create
a final harmonious wish:
all of it together is work.
If you want to make a show about Runaways—
you have to know it's a job.
Sweat is the real proof.

In rage
trying to get away
the worst pain
is remembering
a pleasant smell
(fresh baked bread, soap)
or a joke or a squeeze or
to admit to
an unexpected pleasure
a present
from those you would have loved fiercely—
but now run from.

S**top**—search your brain
for a postcard in a scrapbook
an old love.
You *did* love
and that
hurts your case.
A runaway must have
expected something
or he or she wouldn't
have been disappointed.

And expectations come from
the hint of something whispered
maybe in a lullaby
right after you were born.
A quiet private song
between a baby and a stranger
that said
life could be good somehow
life could be good.

Runaways

RUNAWAYS was first performed at The New York Shakespeare Festival Public Theater on March 9, 1978. It was written, composed and directed by Elizabeth Swados. Settings were by Douglas W. Schmidt and Woods Mackintosh, costumes by Hilary Rosenfeld, and lighting by Jennifer Tipton. The producer was Joseph Papp. The cast was as follows:

HUBBELL . . . . .Bruce Hlibok

A. J. . . . . .Anthony Imperato

JACKIE . . . . .Diane Lane
also played by Rachel Kelly

LIDIA . . . . .Jossie De Guzman

MELINDA . . . . .Trini Alvarado

NIKKI KAY KANE . . . . .Nan-Lynn Nelson

MANNY . . . . .Randy Ruiz

EDDIE . . . . .Jon Matthews

SUNDAR . . . . .Bernie Allison

ROBY .Venustra K. Robinson

LAZAR . . . . .David Schechter

ERIC . . . . .Evan Miranda

IGGY . . . . .Jonathan Feig

DEIDRE . . . . .Karen Evans

EZ . . . . .Leonard (Duke) Brown

LUIS . . . . .Ray Contreras

MEX-MONGO . . . . .Mark Anthony Butler

JANE . . . . .Kate Schellenbach

INTERPRETER FOR HUBBELL . . . .Lorie Robinson

CHORUS . . . . .Sheila Gibbs, Toby Parker

PIANO AND TOY PIANO . . . . .Judith Fleisher

STRING BASS .John Schimmel

CONGAS, TIMBALES, BONGOS, BELLS
   SIREN AND OTHERS . . . . . . .Leopoldo F. Fleming

TRAP SET, TRIANGLE, GLASS AND
   RATCHET . . . . .David Sawyer

SAXOPHONES AND FLUTES . . . . .Patience Higgins

GUITAR . . . . .Elizabeth Swados

Act I

You Don't Understand
I Had to Go
Parent/Kid Dance
Appendectomy
Where Do People Go
Footsteps
Once Upon a Time
Current Events
Every Now and Then
Out on the Street
Minnesota Strip
Song of a Child Prostitute
Christmas Puppies
Que Si que Quieres
    Sera una Puta
Game Chant
Lazar's Heroes
Find Me a Hero
Scrynatchkielooaw
The Undiscovered Son
I Went Back Home
This Is What I Do When
   I'm Angry
The Basketball Song
Spoons
Lullaby for Luis
Goodnight Mommy
We Are Not Strangers

Act II

In the Sleeping Line
Lullaby from Baby to
   Baby
Tra Gog Vo in Dein
   Whole
Revenge Song
Enterprise
Sometimes
Clothes
We Are Not Strangers
   II (Reggae)
Mr. Graffiti
The Untrue Pigeon
Señoras de la Noche
We Have to Die?
Where Are Those
   People Who Did *Hair*?
Appendectomy II
Let Me Be a Kid
To the Dead of Family
   Wars
Problem After Problem
Lonesome of the Road
Let Me Be a Kid
   (Reprise)

ACT I

All of Runaways *takes place in the same playground with benches, fence, bleachers, and a basketball hoop.*

You Don't Understand

*Hubbell is deaf. He checks the dark playground to
make sure it's safe. He opens the fence door cautiously
and enters. He signs to the audience, and his interpreter speaks.*

HUBBELL:
Just ran away. I had to run away.
My parents can hear, but I can't,
and they blame me for that.
I didn't do anything. I can't speak their
language, and they can't speak mine.
I need a place . . . to hide . . . to feel safe.
Can you help me? Can you?
Of course you can't.

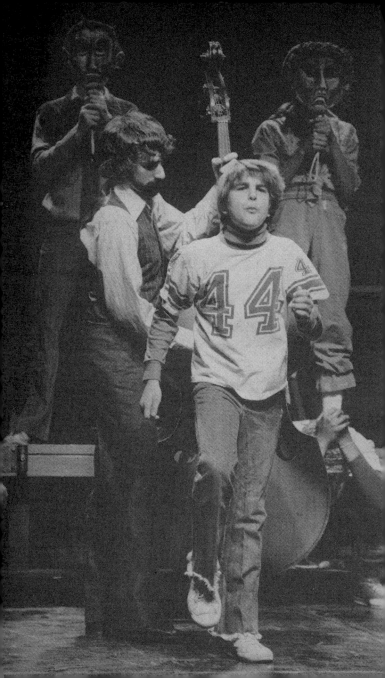

I Had to Go

A. J. dashes onto the stage as if being chased by a siren. The bass player from the band stands behind him, looming over him. Three actors with parent masks stand above him on a platform. A. J. speaks to the audience.

A. J.:
My parents lived together, but they hated each other. See, my father went to work, see, he was the head of the family. And Mom, it was her job to stay home all day and clean the house. And every night at about six o'clock, I'd hear the electric garage door open, and I'd think to myself: "Did I do everything right? Did I do everything right?" Then I'd hear him come up the stairs. This was it! Please don't yell, Dad. Please don't yell. Then Mom would call us, and we'd all go sit at the table. And there'd be silence, until my father would say something stupid. And my mother would break down and they'd start fighting, and she'd grab us and put our coats on and try to take us out the door, and my father would pull us back in and leave my mother out on the porch all by herself. And I was tired of being fought over. I had to go! I had to go!

The bass player slaps the bass six times like it's A. J.'s face.

Parent/Kid Dance

*Everyone comes on running to the drums. They run
from different dangers. They form lines, running faster
and faster in place, and try to push away what scares
them.*

LAZAR:
Faster! Faster! HELP!

Everyone sits, hugging knees, heads down.

Appendectomy

Jackie comes on with a doll and her own form of medicine kit. While she sings she gives an anesthetic with a bicycle pump, cuts open the doll with cuticle scissors, and removes poisons with a spoon. Band-Aids and thread are also important for healing.

JACKIE:
This is very serious.
It looks like this child has been severely beaten.

We'll have to perform an appendectomy.
Please give her anesthetic.
The nail scissors please.
The toilet paper please.
Now the rubber bands please.
It looks as if this child has got a broken heart.
The straw for breathing please.
Ssshh. I must have absolute quiet.
What are these terrible bruises on her back?
We must report this at once.
The vaseline please.
I've made a perfect incision.
We must remove the infection at once.
She's saying: "Mommy, Mommy."
She doesn't know that her mother is locked up in
    Bellevue for observation.
But we mustn't tell our children.
We must protect our children as much as possible.
It's lucky for her I came along.
These parents who won't watch their children's
    appendixes.
They'll have me doing brain surgery next.
Now let's hook her up to this life-saving device,
And keep all her vital functions going.
In the meantime,
I'll have to plant a quarter and a secret message
    inside her stomach.
Just from me to her
And that will make her safe, completely safe,
'Cause I'll always be inside of her.
The needle and thread please.
We're going to stitch her up now.
And when she heals,
No one will ever know what's inside of her,
Except of course me.
And she can always show her scars to everyone.
See?

Jackie holds the doll out to the audience, showing her
scar, as the music starts for the next number.

Where Do People Go

*The Runaways transform their loneliness into games.
They play in circles, in twos and fours, and finally
dance together in an incredible imaginary disco.*

LUIS:
eeny meeny gipsaleeny
ooh aah combaleeny
ooh mamacha cucaracha
C O D

**HUBBELL AND A.J. AND ALL WHITE MEMBERS
OF COMPANY:**
engine, engine number nine
goin' down Chicago line
if the train falls off the track
do you want your money back
yes or no
odds or evens, odds or evens

**ROBY AND MEX-MONGO AND ALL BLACK
MEMBERS OF COMPANY:**
eeny meeny miny mo
catch a nigger by the toe
if he hollers let him go
eeny meeny miny mo

**LUIS AND LIDIA AND ALL HISPANIC MEMBERS
OF COMPANY:**
tin marín de dos pinguéy
cúcara mácara títre fué
cuantas patas tiene un gato
una dos tres y cuatro

**LUIS, LIDIA, ROBY,
MEX, HUBBELL, A.J.:**
Where do people go
When they run away?

COMPANY
(simultaneously):
duck, duck, duck, duck
duck, duck, duck, duck
goose, goose, goose,
  goose

Tell me where do they go
And where do they stay
    if they stay?

Do they find themselves
    a television in the
    waiting room of the
    nearest train station,
    bus station, runaway
    house or community
    center?
And turn on the screen
    and sit watching and
    waiting—I wonder for
    what?

duck, duck, duck, duck
duck, duck, duck, duck
goose, goose, goose,
    goose

A tisket, a tasket, a green
    and yellow basket
I wrote a letter to my
    mother and on the way
    I dropped it.
I dropped it, I dropped it,

    and on the way I
    dropped it.

A tisket, a tasket, a green
    and yellow basket.
I wrote a letter to my
    mother and on the way
    I dropped it.

Now tell me
Where do people go
When they run away?
Tell me, where do they
    go,
And what do they say to
    each other?

duck, duck, duck, duck
duck, duck, duck, duck
goose, goose, goose,
    goose

Are they chickens
    together on Forty-
    second Street?
Or seatmates together in
    boarding school in
    Massachusetts?
Or are they on line
    together at the abor-
    tion office at the
    community center?

Concentration (*snap,
    snap*)
Categories (*snap, snap*)
Names of (*snap, snap*)
Subway stops (*snap,
    snap*)

Concentration (*snap,
    snap*)
Categories (*snap, snap*)

It's all the same when
  you're lonely.

Names of (*snap, snap*)
Restaurants (*snap, snap*)

Concentration (*snap,
  snap*)
Categories (*snap, snap*)
Names of (*snap, snap*)
Disco bars (*snap, snap*)

COMPANY:
Where do people go
When they run away?
Tell me where do they go,
And where do they stay if they stay?

Do they sit in the movies all day like sad old men?
Do they go to the factory and work their asses off?
Do they go to political meetings and shout their
  problems out?
Do they leave home and then go back home, mothers
  and fathers do that a lot.
Do they go from relative to relative to foster home to
  foster home to theatre groups to therapy to jogging
  to long walks and long talks and arguments and
  reconciliations?
It's all the same when you're lonely.

**LIDIA, LUIS,
MELINDA:**

Where do people go
When they run away?
Tell me where do they go,
And where do they stay
  if they stay?

Dónde uno va
Cuando se fuga?
Dime dónde va?

Will they stay with anyone who'll take them?
Hoping and waiting
Hoping and waiting
Hoping and waiting,
ESPERANDO!

Footsteps

Nikki kneels down. The bass player comes and hovers over her. She pleads with the audience. She tells of her scary nights. The other Runaways sit with their heads on their knees.

NIKKI:
Footsteps, I remember footsteps.
Carpet, on the carpet in the living room,
My room was down the hall.
Every night before I went to bed, I'd check the closet,
For the people hiding in my pants and shoes,
And in my slippers and my nightgown,
I would turn on the hall light
And count the cars that rushed by the curve.
My house was on a curve.
Did my father's car have a low-sounding motor?
And when they slammed the door it would go: one, two—
My father's slam, my mother's, then the key would click.
The door.
And then the footsteps, blessed footsteps on the carpet
Waiting for the footsteps coming toward my room.
Just checking on the baby
Making sure she's sound asleep.
Screaming, fighting, yelling with the door closed.
Oh my God, I thought.
Do they know I'm wide awake and is that why they're fighting?
Mother's voice was very low and provocative,
"Don't wake the kid up." And father screaming in hysterics,
"I'm not waking any kid up." And so on and so forth.
And then the footsteps, careful footsteps on the carpet.
Just to check and see if I'd heard anything.
Oh no, I didn't hear it.
I just want to hear a story

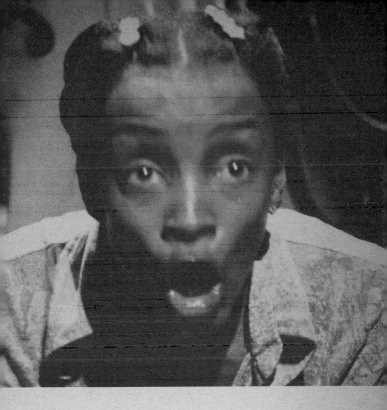

Or have a stomachache
Or did you bring me any presents?
And then goodnight and prayers, and endless prayers
That I'll bless anyone just so I don't have to
Go to sleep, goodnight.
Must check the closet, you can never tell who's
    sneaking in the ceiling,
You never can tell who hides weapons in my loafers,
Poison in my Levi's, monsters in the bureau drawers,
And nightmares, all night long I'm hearing footsteps.
Who's coming down the hall to eat me?
All night long I'm hearing footsteps,
Gritting my teeth and making outrageous promises to
    God

To do all kinds of jobs in his service
If I can just make it 'till morning. Footsteps
Footsteps Footsteps leave me alone!

The bass player slaps his bass three times like it's
Nikki's face. Everyone feels the blows. As the bass is
slapped, Lidia and Luis start to argue in Spanish.

LIDIA:	Tu no estabas aquí anoche. Dónde estabas tu anoche?
LUIS:	A tí no te importa. Yo estaba afuera.
LIDIA:	A mí sí me importa. Afuera? A dónde afuera?
LUIS:	Vacilando con los muchachos.
LIDIA:	Muchachos ó muchacha.
LUIS:	Yo dije muchachos.
LIDIA:	No te creo.
LUIS:	No me creas.
LIDIA:	No te creo.
LUIS:	No seas estúpida.
LIDIA:	Estúpido tu.
LUIS:	Déjame tranquilo.
LIDIA:	Vete al infierno.
LUIS:	Tu primero.
LIDIA:	Contigo encima.
LUIS:	Sucia.
LIDIA:	Idiota.
LUIS:	Basura.
LIDIA:	Imberbe.
LUIS:	Bruta.
LIDIA:	Aprovechao.
LUIS:	Puta.
LIDIA:	Cabrón.
LUIS:	Cabrona.
LIDIA:	Tu madre.
LUIS:	Cachapera.
LIDIA:	Abusador.
LUIS:	Apestosa.
LIDIA:	Lambío.

Once Upon a Time

While the "once upon a time" story is being told, three couples of boys and girls walk and walk in place, getting nowhere. They get exhausted. They try to comfort one another. Then they fight. The story ends with a scream.

LIDIA: Once upon a time,
There was a boy or a girl
Who ran far away from home.

LIDIA AND ERIC: He or she had to run because
He or she got into a lot of fights.

COMPANY: He or she was nine or twelve or six years old.

He or she never laughed when anyone was looking.

He or she ate food out of garbage cans and shoplifted from grocery stores.

He or she never admitted that he or she was born.

LIDIA: He or she said that he or she just got here.

COMPANY: He or she said that he or she just got here.

LIDIA: People would pick him or her up
And he or she would sell pamphlets and books for them.

COMPANY: Once, he or she had to be a prostitute.

Once, he or she had to stick himself or herself with a needle.

LIDIA: Whenever he or she tried to go home,

	His or her mother or father would beat him or her up,
COMPANY:	Or his or her mother or father would not see him or her,
LIDIA:	Or he or she would get locked out.
COMPANY:	So the boy or girl became invisible, And magical. And he or she would turn into whatever kept him or her alive.
LIDIA:	And nothing scared him or her.

COMPANY: Therefore this twelve or nine or six-year-old little boy or girl was never no longer a child.
He or she never admitted that he or she was born.
He or she said that he or she just got here.
He or she said that he or she just got here.
And he or she never laughed when anyone was looking,
And he or she never cried.
And this is not the end.
The End.
Aaaaah. . . .

Current Events

Eddie comes forward facing the audience and tries to give his current events report for social studies class. He gets it confused with his own unhappy home life and starts to cry.

EDDIE:
Today is my day to make
A report for current events.
Do you have current events?
It's part of my social studies class and involves the
news of the day.
And what the newspapers say.
I'd like to start my paragraph
By stating that the headlines have hurt my feelings
And that today is an especially
discouraging summary of facts.
I feel like crying and please don't flunk me.
Things simply go like this,
They're working on a neutron bomb
That will preserve buildings and exterminate human
life,
Slowly and scientifically,
With radiation sickness, but please don't flunk me.
A cop killed a kid who threatened him with a toy gun
and got six years,
And soon will be up for probation,
But please don't flunk me.
And in the blackout this summer at least seven people
were killed,
And no one's admitted it to anyone.
More people died this year in family murders
Than in all the battles in Northern Ireland.
And a pretty brunette is writing
Letters of love to the Son of Sam.
And though I'm not political you know,
I am scared, for this crazy heart of mine keeps
pounding wildly.
Like I've just run an especially long distance
Or had a dream that I can't remember.
Please don't flunk me.
These are current events:
At eight fifty-five Monday evening my father hit my
mother across her mouth.
They're kidnapping people all over the world.
Patty Hearst went crazy and got free.

In Detroit there's a crazy guy who's shooting kids in
     the face.
Oh Mom, don't let that happen to me.
My brother cracked up my father's Buick.
In Bronx State Hospital a junkie killed his shrink.
There are no more air-raid drills 'cause it won't matter.
And all these books are coming out and saying
That the C.I.A. killed Kennedy,
The F.B.I., Martin Luther King.
Kennedy tried to kill Castro.
I usually don't think about these things.
I play baseball or make models in my room,
But it's current events and you're asking me.
And my parents are becoming a statistic: a divorce.
And I am becoming a statistic: a fucked-up kid.
And a pretty brunette is sending love letters to the
     Son of Sam,
And though I'm not political,
I hear the Shah of Iran cuts off people's hands.
And when I play my guitar,
Sometimes my fingers turn numb and I get this pain in
     my gut.
And I ask myself, What am I working so hard for?
Just to be a statistic?
I'm scared and that's current events.
Helter Skelter's a bestseller,
Snipers are everywhere on the roofs.
I read yesterday that prostitution has become pros-
     perous around Disneyland,
And a crazy guy in Detroit is shooting kids in the face,
And more family murders have taken place in the last
     year
Than in all of Northern Ireland,
And I don't want my family to die.
And that's today's especially discouraging summary
     of facts,
And I feel like crying,
But please don't flunk me.
Please don't flunk me.

Every Now and Then

As A.J. and the rest sing, Sundar does a slow ballet around the playground on his skateboard. His skateboard is all he has. Sometimes he almost loses his balance from loneliness. Mex-Mongo hangs from the basketball hoop. Nikki tries to skateboard without a skateboard. No one pays attention to anyone else. Everyone's lonely.

A.J.:	Every now and then a person has to get away,
	Even from those he loves.
	How he goes or who he hurts,
	Can not matter at the time.
COMPANY:	He's leaving.
EZ:	Oh oh I'm sorry,
	I think I was inconsiderate.
	I made you worry,
	Without even thinking about it.
COMPANY:	Every now and then a choice gets made,
	And some debt in your heart won't be paid.
	Who gets left behind no one knows.
	Don't always condemn the one who goes.
EZ, LIDIA, MELINDA:	Oh oh I'm sorry,
	I think I was inconsiderate.
	I made you worry,
	Without even thinking about it.
COMPANY:	Every time I look back I have regrets
	I know I should leave behind.
EZ, LIDIA, MELINDA:	Make no further excuses for me,
	I had to do it this way.
COMPANY:	Oh oh I'm sorry,
	I think I was inconsiderate.
	I made you worry,
	Without even thinking about it.

Out on the Street

Hubbell signs to the audience, and his interpreter speaks.

HUBBELL:

When you're out on the street, you're all alone, you
know you're all alone.

People don't see you, but you do see people.

And when people do see you, it's because they want
you.

They don't care who you are. It's you, your body that
they want.

And once they're finished using it, they throw it away,

Just like trash.

Out there, you've gotta walk, you've gotta walk.

And the people, the cars, the buildings, the street, and
the sky—

Everything's looking down on you, and you feel
oppressed and overwhelmed.

And you become scared, scared of yourself.

Minnesota Strip

During Hubbell's speech, Jackie and Manny have appeared at the top of a ramp at the back of the playground. They come down slowly as Roby sings. The Runaways get tense. They know the pimp and his child prostitute are dangerous stuff. He's holding her half like she's his lover, half like she's his prisoner.

ROBY:
Let me tell you about the
  Minnesota Strip.

MEX-MONGO:
Hey!

ROBY:
The big men come and
  they make the little
  kids trip.

MEX-MONGO:
Hey! Hey!

ROBY:
They fill their brains
  with drugs and then,

MEX-MONGO:
Hey! Hey! Hey!

ROBY:
They make them lie
  down with their
  money-paying men.

ROBY, LIDIA, EZ:
Stay away, stay away
  from the Minnesota Strip.
Stay away, stay away
  from the Minnesota Strip.

EZ (*simultaneously*):
The people and
the cars and
the trucks and
the trains and
the planes are
the noises and
the sounds that
I hate.

LUIS:
(*Spanish chant*)

Song of a Child Prostitute

Everyone leaves except the older prostitutes, who are angry about the new girl on their turf. When Jackie sings she seems half asleep. She feels almost nothing. The pimp never lets go of her.

JACKIE:

No one treats me like Mico do.
He buys me halter tops and corkies,
And he got me a waterbed up on our flat on Avenue C
    between Fifth and Sixth.
He built gratings and he has a shepard named Duke so
    we're safe.
All Mico says is that we live in a free generation
And the man and the woman go into mutual enterprise,
And sex is a business like kitchenware,
Lucrative, prosperous and even humanitarian.
If some middle-aged dude is freaking out because he
    can't get along with his family,
I can make him feel like a daddy.
I can make him feel like a daddy.
Mico says a lay is a game.
When I was a kid and my parents would check on me
    before they'd shoot up,
And I'd pretend to be asleep.
Mico says it's the same.
Just pretend you feel good.
Just pretend you feel good.
Mostly everything works like clockwork,
And I'll be Mico's number one girl forever,
Or at least until I'm sixteen and can get my learner's
    permit,
To drive to Montana to be a rancher.
But for now it's not bad at seven minutes a stretch,
To be someone's dolly,
To be someone's daughter,
To be someone's sister,
To pretend to be glad,
To pretend to be glad.
If the digital stopwatch that Mico bought me keeps
    working,
I stay out of trouble.
Legs open at one and close at seven,
And I'm safe 'cause Mico steals pills from a medical
    warehouse.
I open at one minute, close at seven.

If I ever go overtime, I catch hell.
Once I met a guy, he was a sailor.
He was eighteen,
He had acne, he was very sweet, he didn't do anything.
He asked me if I could go to Ohio and live with his
   mother.
When I asked Mico, he laughed at me.
He said there'd be no more waterbed.
No more grass, no more pills in bright colors.
He said I couldn't ever be number one again.
How could I be after I hurt him so bad?
He needs me.
He needs me.
He's made a deal to reward me. He's raising my
   percentage.
He met a producer and I'll go in the movies.
I'm only thirteen and I can still go naked.
And the men who touch me,
They're college type actors.
I'll pretend I'm a movie star.
I'll pretend I'm an actress.
I'll pretend I'm a college bowl queen.

Christmas Puppies

---

*Nikki is angry about her turf being invaded. She
pushes Jackie out of the way and speaks to the audience.*

NIKKI:
Did you ever see those packs of dogs that's made up of
   everybody's old Christmas puppies?
And then they just end up roamin' around the street
   looking for garbage.
It's not the dogs' fault.
You know, like, they didn't ask to have the little rib-
bons tied around their necks for Christmas.

And they didn't ask to be let out of cars on street
  corners.
But you watch those packs of strays.
It's real interesting the way they go around together
  playing like they're teammates or something.
But the truth is—each one is out for hisself.
And if one of the puppies starts bleeding, like he
Gets himself hit by a car or cut on a bottle or somethin',
  then ow ooow,
Better watch out 'cause those other dogs'll just leave
  him there in the street
All alone to bleed and howl and worse, there's
  somethin' they do that's really disgusting.
Like, if the pack is super hungry. . . .
But I don't have to say it.
And there's nobody to blame in all of this.
'Cause hunger is hunger, you know?

Que Si que Quieres
Ser una Puta

The older Hispanic prostitute curses Jackie out in Spanish. Everyone comes to the fences and joins in. They say, "It's her choice to be a whore—she could say yes or no." As they mock, Nikki pulls Jackie's head back from behind, while Manny pushes an imaginary pill into her mouth.

LIDIA:
Que si que quieres ser una puta.
Si quieres ser puta,
Entonces haz lo que estás haciendo.
Pretende ser joven e inocente.
Y que lo que haces no es tu culpa.
Luego como una pequeña vaca estúpida, y actúa escandalizada cuando te agolpean brutalmente
    pero tu no me engañas pequeña puta
Yo he estado aquí demasiado tiempo
Una persona puede decir sí
Una persona puede decir no
y tu sabes la decisión que has tomado.

Game Chant

Manny lifts Jackie from the floor and swings her around and around in a violent, fast circle, like a terrible game.

COMPANY (*simultaneously*):
eeny meeny gipsaleeny
ooh aah combaleeny
ooh mamacha cucaracha
C O D

eeny meeny miny mo
catch a piggy by the toe
if he hollers let him go
eeny meeny miny mo

tín marín de dos pinguéy
cúcara mácara títre fué
cuantas patas tiene un gato
una dos tres y cuatro

engine, engine number nine
goin' down Chicago line
if the train falls off the track
do you want your money back

ooo, aoo, beep, beep, walkin' down the street
ten times a week with your funky feet
oongawa, oongawa, this is black power
destroy white boy. I said it, I meant it.

Manny puts Jackie down. She collapses to the floor, holding her head.

Una persona puede decír sí
Una persona puede decír no.

Lazar's Heroes

This scene is too heavy. Lazar comes on carrying a suitcase, dressed in a frock coat and red tap shoes. He is going to lighten things up with his version of a Vaudeville and Truth act. He tells us that all we have seen happened because there are no more heroes. He gives us the history of comic books and then brings on Lazar's Marching Band to make the show more accessible to adults: finally we have costumes and musical-comedy choreography.

LAZAR:
Hey, hey,
Who is directing this movie?
The sound track is all wrong, all wrong.
It's too gloomy. It's too savage.
We need some violins.
Something more upbeat.
People will not wait in line for two hours unless they
can go out humming something upbeat.
And who is editing this thing?
It's all choppy and black and white.
Nothing is black and white.
We need some Technicolor, or Vistavision,
Some Sensurround.
What this movie needs is a hero.
But there are no more heroes.
Do you know why there are no more heroes?
It's because when George Washington decided to
found this country,
He went to Washington, D.C.,
Which at that time was swarming with superheroes.
There were so many superheroes, he had to get rid of
them so that he could build the Capitol.
So he rented a printing press,
And he lured all the superheroes into the printing press,
And he flattened them out. Just flattened them out.
And that's why there are D.C. comics.
It's all those flattened-out superheroes stapled
together.
And there were so many that they had to build the
Library of Comics.
And I have evidence. I have proof.
The Spectacular Spiderman, flattened out.
Superman, flattened out.
The Incredible Hulk, flattened out.
Every superhero is flattened out.
And now it's time to tap dance.

Find Me a Hero

COMPANY (*Hubbell signing*):	Find me a hero. Make the old fairytales come true. Put him on a horsey. Give him a shield and a crown. Find me a hero.
LAZAR:	Don't mean no sandwich So many different variations of unhappy endings are coming my way, I think I've got me a Lancelot and then I clap my hands and he's gone away.
COMPANY:	Find me a hero. Make the old fairytales come true. Put him on a skateboard. Give him a shield and a crown. Find me a hero.
LAZAR:	Don't mean no Blimpie. I want him to be President, yes. I want him to be a winner. Walking with a marching band, And I won't accept a sinner.
COMPANY:	Find me a hero. Make the old fairytales come true. Put him on a moped. Give him some gloves and a helmet. Find me a hero.
LAZAR:	Don't mean no meatloaf.
COMPANY:	Hero, hero, I want a hero. Make me a hero, don't let me down.

	Find me a reason. Give me a leader. Give me confidence. Don't let me down.
	Hero, hero, I want a hero. Make me a hero, don't let me down.
	Find me a reason. Give me a leader. Give me confidence. Don't let me down.
A.J.:	Don't want him sad. Don't want confusion.
ALL:	Don't want that boring preaching, or false conclusions.
A.J.:	Don't want no bitterness or violent action.
ALL:	No easy answers. No quick reactions.

Iggy takes a violin solo, deadpan.

ALL:	Find me a hero. Make the old fairytales come true. Put him on a horsey. Give him a shield and a crown. Find me a hero. Find me a hero. Find me a hero.

YEE HAH!

Scrynatchkielooaw

Nikki comes forward wearing a necklace of holy orna-ments and doing a high-stepping ritual walk. She con-fides to the air—or whoever is listening—about her incredible religion that solves everything. She demon-strates some of the ways she prays.

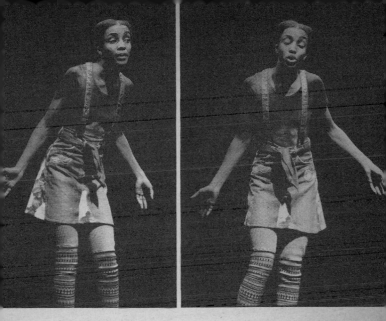

NIKKI:
SCRYNATCHKIELOOAW NO NI NING SHAKA-
BUTSO HINE HO HEE YA KIKOBATSO HAI!

You are in the middle of a very holy person. Me.
See, I am studying a religion that teaches me to be
super-peaceful and real generous to everybody and it
will also prepare me for death. Now this is what I do.
I take a step forward and then I say this secret ancient
word—*scrynatchkielooaw*—and then I jump up and
down, up and down (you know—heaven, hell, heaven,
hell). And my mouth has to constantly open and close
so that I can give out all sorts of real important infor-
mation. See, see, what I am is a dummy, and God is
my ventriloquist and we sorta have this act we do together and what I am is his big wooden doll and God
throws his voice into me. Throw that voice, God. Now
some people may call this copping out, but if you're
born a dummy, you're born a dummy and there ain't
nothin' you can do about it.

The Undiscovered Son

*Eric is a spoiled brat. But he has nothing. So he fanta-
sizes that he is a spoiled brat and acts out all the
gestures and dances of the famous people he'd like to
be related to. He lies on a wood platform like it's a
chaise lounge. The bass player is at his feet; the pianist
plays a toy piano at his head: imaginary Mom and
Dad.*

ERIC (*spoken*):
I am the undiscovered son of Judy Garland
And I can sing and dance and wear fancy clothes.
And whereas my sister Liza has to really work for
    applause
All you have to do is look at me
And you weep with standing ovations.
I am the unknown son of John F. Kennedy.
I am incredibly good-looking and smart as hell.
After I graduate from Harvard, Yale and Princeton
I will run for Mayor and then who knows.
I own a horse and three large dogs.
I am the undiscovered son of Eddie Fisher.
I can croon and make your mother's heart melt.
Also me and my sister Carrie are starring in a new
    science-fiction movie where I conquer and destroy a
    four-story man-eating robot.

Do you want to get married in the White House today?
My father says it's OK.
Do you want to get married in the White House today?
My father says it's OK.

I am the son of Pelé, the favorite nephew of Reggie
    Jackson, the first cousin of O. J. Simpson and the
    godson of Kareem Abdul-Jabbar.
Muhammad Ali has built a guest bedroom just for me.
I am the undiscovered son of the Ali Kahn.
He was a prince or something.

Now I'm a prince or something too.
I have a sister who was named after a flower.
I was named after a sunset. My name is Prince Sunset
  or something.

Do you want to get married in the White House today?
My father says it's OK.
Do you want to get married in the White House today?
My father says it's OK.

MARLON BRANDO! MARILYN MONROE! JEAN
SIMMONS! ENGLEBERT HUMPERDINCK!
GEORGE WASHINGTON! DINAH SHORE!
CATHERINE DENOUVIER!

I Went Back Home

Iggy is bored. When Eric is finished showing off, he sulks on and kicks a trash can, then lights a match, throws it in and watches the can ignite. He stands as close to the flames as he can and talks about himself. He speaks in a dull, flat tone. He's been through so much—nothing impresses him. In the background, Roby vocalizes "Lullabye from Baby to Baby" throughout Iggy's speech.

IGGY:

I went back home and they were sitting by the TV watching "As the World Turns" and they just pretended that I wasn't there, and they know that really gets to me. "Do you smell a nobody in the room?" says my father to my mother. I went back home and they ignored me because they know it makes me crazy. I mean, it's not like I haven't been missing for ten days. I clear my throat and my mother turns up the TV and my father belches, blaapp.

So I decide to do what I always do when I want to get their attention. I kick in the glass on the TV and I bend the antennas back like little rabbit ears and I say, "TV is for Polish Russian morons." So my father picks me up in the air and throws me onto the floor. And his face is close to mine and the liquor smells like love on his breath. And he calls me a bastard but at least he's talking to me and my mother picks up the broken TV glass off the floor, talking to it and weeping like it's an injured child and things are going good now so I tell them that they are stupid, uneducated assholes and they scream, "You need a bath." And I scream, "You need some brains." So my mother starts boiling the water on the stove and my father is ripping the clothes off my back and they throw me into the bathtub and my mother pours the boiling water on my back and my father scrapes the dirt off my back with the glass from the TV. And they say, "This will teach you to come home."

I went back home and they were sitting by the TV watching "As the World Turns" and they pretended that I wasn't there. So I had to let them know, you know.

This Is What I Do When I'm Angry

Screams. Some kids get furious at their loneliness. They've climbed high on the bleachers. They punch at the sky and yell at the top of their lungs.

A.J. AND NIKKI:
It's not my fault, it's not my fault.
Check it out!
This is what I do when I'm angry.
I break windows.
First I check to make sure that the window is close-ed.
Then I pull down the shade.
Just to pull it down.
Then I raise the shade.
Then I check the window again.
To make sure that everything is all right.
And then I take my fist.
And I pull it back as far as I can.
And I get real strong.
And I shove my hand through the glass.

COMPANY:
eeny meeny miny mo
catch a piggy by the toe
if he hollers, let him go
eeny meeny miny mo
odds or evens
yes or no
yes or no
yes or no

The Basketball Song

EZ brings life back onto the playground at its darkest moment. He shows how he survives, how his basketball gives him magical powers. His dancing with the group begins as an excited team workout and ends in a passionate African circle dance where everyone gets blessed with basketballs, drums and shakers.

EZ:
Here in these hands I hold a planet,
Bigger than the sun and stranger than the moon.
When my mom is sad and hating me I play basketball.
Come on y'all.

COMPANY:
Here in these hands I hold a planet,
Bigger than the sun and stranger than the moon.
When my mom is sad and hating me I play basketball.

EZ:
And in the afternoon when my father's out looking for
  a kid to beat,
I hide here in this, a holy court, and I dribble with the
  heads of kings. Yeah.

COMPANY:
Here in these hands I hold a magic ball,
And I can look in it and see me.
I run past laughter, I jump from pain,
I shoot the moon into a black hole and because of my
  aim,

EZ:
You have the moonlight and the tide.

COMPANY:
Yea, yea, the moonlight and the tide.

EZ:
You have the moonlight and the tide.

COMPANY:
Yea, yea, the moonlight and the tide.

EZ:	**GIRLS:**
Here in these hands I've got a dinosaur's ball.	Shoot, shoot, shoo do do do
Potent in its manly strength	Shoot, shoot, shoo do do do
Making history on my team and deadly in its aim	Shoot, shoot, shoo do do do In its aim yea.

COMPANY:	**GIRLS:**
Here in these hands I have the eye of a giant,	Shoot, shoot, shoo do do do
The head of a pirate, a million-karat ruby	Shoot, shoot, shoo do do do
I shoot them all into their big black holes:	

EZ:
Venus, Mars, Uranus, Pluto, Jupiter and due to my aim,

GIRLS:
Well.

EZ:
You have the planets and the stars.

GIRLS:
Yea, yea, planets and stars.

EZ:
You have the planets and the stars.

GIRLS:
Yea, yea, planets and stars.

LAZAR:
One, two, three, four, five, six . . .
Doubletime.
Play ball.

The energy of the basketball dance explodes. Luis goes wild and takes out his knife. First he dances around the basketball, and then he falls to the floor and stabs it again and again. He is furious. He collapses from his rage.

Spoons

Manny is a pusher. He's so quiet you can hardly hear him. He can see Luis is an easy mark. He takes his spoon and puts it to Luis's arm. He stabs Luis three times with the spoon, and Luis starts to nod out. He might O.D.

MANNY:
A long time ago I used to take the spoon from my breakfast cereal and whammo, throw it up against the wall and watch the milk and the cornflakes dribble, dribble, dribble. And I'd laugh, you know, and wait for someone to come and pick up that spoon and give it back to me. But no one ever did. I was in one of them high-efficiency orphanages, and the cleaning lady would curse and mop up the mess. And some gray-striped volunteer would just plop another spoon into my bowl. Bang and I'd whammo whirl it up in the air again like a military helicopter and I'd throw it up against the wall and the cleaning ladies would keep cleaning up my spoon and the cornflakes and another spoon would keep being plopped in my bowl. No one ever tried to talk to me about it not ever. No one had the time to put a hand on my shoulder and say—stop it, little kid. I'm always fascinated by the fact that if you drop something and no one picks it up you forget you ever dropped it. Maybe that's why I feel I can just float away any time. Maybe that's why the spoon game got boring. Anyway, I play with spoons now too. I fill them with the double eagle, horse, white powder, heroin, and I melt them over candles. And no one stops me now either. Now I'm in an orphanage for grownups. The world. The world is an orphanage for grownups. And I'm a pusher. So my name gets put on the blue clipboard for the bad boys instead of on the white one for the good.

Lullaby for Luis

Lidia slaps Luis again and again. She tries to dress him in his prom tuxedo and remind him of all the good that could happen if he'd get off junk. She tries to keep him alive by dancing him awake. She revives him; he collapses; she revives him; he collapses. Finally he dies. She screams. The sax player has been onstage the whole time trying to lift Luis up with his tones. He screams.

LIDIA:
Canción de coma Luis.
  Canción de coma Luis.
Canción de coma Luis.
  Canción de coma Luis.
No lullabies for Luis
  boy,
He's gonna take a walk,
Right here through his
  rich Puerto Rican
  garden,
Out onto the veranda
Look at the snapdragons
  with their wild
  tongues.

	LUIS (*simultaneously*):
No lullabies for Luis boy	You don't want me to sleep now do you?
He's gonna keep on walking,	Gonna keep on walking,
Right through his royal terrace	Right through his royal terrace
The orchestra is playing a mambo	The orchestra is playing a mambo
The president's wife would like to dance with you.	The president's wife would like to dance with me.

COMPANY:
Walk, Luis, dance, Luis,
   walk, walk, walk,
Walk, Luis, dance, Luis,
   walk, walk, walk.

LIDIA:
How handsome you is in   Thank you
   your white tuxedo and
   your white patent
   leather shoes.   Patent leather shoes

No lullabies for Luis boy   You don't want me to
                                   sleep now do you?

He's walking on the   Walking on the moon
   moon   like an astronaut.
One step for you to stay
   awake
And one step for man-   Like on the TV
   kind.
Watch out for them
   craters Luis
And the weird little men
   in goggles

LIDIA AND LUIS:
AH, AH, AAHH.

LIDIA:
Walk, first Puerto Rican   I'm walking, first Puerto
   junkie on the moon   Rican astronaut
Walk, first Puerto Rican
   junkie on the moon
Walk, mister astronaut   I'm walking.
   too.
No lullabies, no lullabies   No lullabies, no lullabies
   for you.

COMPANY: No lullabies . . .
Walk, walk, walk, walk,
   walk,

Walk, walk, walk, walk,
    walk,
Walk, walk, walk, walk,
    walk,
Walk, walk, walk, walk,   Ah, ah, ah . . .
    walk,

COMPANY:
Dance with me. Marry   Dance with me.
    me.   Marry me.
Dance with me. Marry   Dance with me.
    me.   Marry me.
All the world is waiting   All the world . . .
    to meet us.
You got to stay awake,   Stay awake . . .
    man.
You can not go to sleep,   Don't go to sleep . . .
    man.
Countries are waiting for   Countries . . .
    you to name them.
Oceans are waiting for   Oceans . . .
    you to cross them.
The sky is waiting to see   Sky . . .
    what kind of weather   Weather . . .
    you want today.
Walk, Luis, stay awake,   Walk, Luis, stay awake,
    Luis.   Luis
Don't go to sleep, Luis.   Walk . . .
Don't leave your
    princess, man.

                                AAAHHH. . . .

The company rushes forward to lift Luis and Lidia up.

Goodnight Mommy

The Runaways are exhausted after a day of fighting for survival. They all go to bed in a line on the floor: it might be a hospital ward, or the floor of a tenement, or perhaps they're dead soldiers. Who knows? Eric whispers a bedtime prayer.

ERIC (*spoken*):

Now you're going to make me kiss you goodnight.
Sometimes you slap me, I don't know why.

There are nights when you're so drunk you even forget I have a bedtime at all, and I stay awake all night and watch TV.
But tonight I have to kiss you goodnight, and pretend like you've been perfect all along.
How can I argue? I'm only twelve.
Anyway,
It's bedtime
Goodnight.
(*kiss*)

LIDIA (*simultaneously sung*):
Brilla, brilla, estrellita

En el cielo pequeñita.
Muy lejos del mundo estás.
Como un diamante en la oscuridad.
Brilla, brilla, estrellita . . .

We Are Not Strangers

COMPANY:
Blow thin wind across the pines.
We have a fire to warm cold hands.
Dusty boots now rest a while.

We are not strangers.

We are not strangers.
We are not strangers.
In fact I know you well.

EZ:
Go to sleep.

LIDIA:
Brilla, brilla, estrellita.

En el cielo pequeñita.

Muy lejos del mundo estás,

Como un diamante en la oscuridad.
Brilla, brilla, estrellita.
En el cielo pequeñita.

Everyone falls back flat into the sleeping line. Blackout.

ACT II

In the Sleeping Line

The Runaways are asleep on stage in the same line when the lights come up. One by one they tell of their nightmares and fears in the night. Some speak quietly. Some jolt up. All are restless, afraid, guilty.

A.J.:
I was walking down Allentown Avenue one night.
And I saw this man.
And I just wanted to walk by him.
As I was walking by him, he walked up to me.
He said: "Do you have any money?"
And I said: "No."
Then he pulled out this huge knife.
And I looked at it and pushed him and he fell.
So I started running.
I didn't know if he was going to get up and chase me again.
There was no one there to save me.

ROBY:
I was coming home from school one night,
And I came the way I usually do along this long block that was badly lit,
And there was this man standing by the school park
And he looked really freaky,
And I wanted to get by him so I could go about my business
And as I walked by him all he said was: "Sinner."
And I looked at him as if to say,
Why are you bothering me? I haven't done anything to you.
But he just kept saying: "Sinner."
And "It started with the blood,
And every month you bleed, you sin."

JACKIE:
I remember the night of my tenth birthday.
We were driving in my mom's car.

She was drunk and I had to drive the car for her.
And I couldn't find the way home.
So this cop car pulled up and said for us
To get in the back seat,
And I told 'em her name.
I felt really awful 'cause the next morning she was
   supposed to hold a big birthday party for me.
And the next morning she really showed up out of the
   jailhouse.
And she'd fixed herself all up.

LAZAR WITH HUBBELL SIGNING:
You know we're all in this major motion picture
   called *The Twentieth Century*,
And the movie is almost over,
And here comes the credits across the screen.
Only there's so many actors in this movie that the
   credits is the New York City phone book,
Where we all get equal billing 'cause we all had bit
   parts.
But that doesn't matter now 'cause the movie's almost
   over,
And this is: THE END.

NIKKI:
Hey, Sundar, you know,
I been meaning to tell you this for a long time now

About how fine you look ridin' on your skateboard,
  you know?
Like I was wondering if maybe . . . (*Deidre pushes her
  back down*)

EDDIE:
Me and my sister had this fight once
But it was weird because I hit her
And I don't usually hit.
But this time I hit her right in the head.
And I got really scared.
So I ran in my room and locked the door.
And I heard the knives coming out in the kitchen,
So I got my knives out.
And all of a sudden,
Knives started hitting my door.
And then one knife came right through my door.
I put my foot against the door.
And finally nothing happened.
In about ten minutes I opened the door and looked in
  the hallway,
And she wasn't there,
So I looked in her room,
And there she was curled up in the corner
Screaming and crying,
"Eddie, Eddie, help me, Eddie.

Mommy doesn't love me, Eddie, she only loves you."
And she was screaming and freaking out.
And I didn't know what to do
And I was so scared because I thought
  I did this to her.
And I went over to her and I hugged her.

LIDIA, LUIS, MANNY (*simultaneously*):
LIDIA:
Una mañana, yo estaba mirando por la ventana
Y de pronto sentí que habia alguien cuando
Miré, habiá un hombre con una cuchilla y
Se estaba acercando y yo grité y nadie
Vino a mi ayuda!

MANNY:
Los otros dias me dijeron que mataron
a mi amigo José. Yo no sé porque
lo mataron, el fué un muchacho muy
bueno, el solamente iba a la iglesia y rezaba mucho.
No sé porque lo mataron.

LUIS:
Mami me voy de la casa
Y voy a cojer un apartmento.
Yo tengo un trabajo y dinero
Puedo hacer lo que yo quiero
Nadie en esta casa me
Respeta por eso que
Me voy y no vengo más.

HUBBEL (*signed*):
Shock!
My God!
That was something creeping up, creeping up.
What should I do?
(*realizes he is not communicating*)
Oh damn it.

Manny sleepwalks to Deidre and falls on his hands over her: rape, murder, we don't know. The whole group wakes simultaneously, screaming.

Lullaby from Baby to Baby

Melinda tries to soothe the Runaways by singing to them. Hubbell and Deidre do gentle hand dances to her song.

MELINDA:
The sun is rising in the
   smoky sky.
The place is any city you
   can name.
In a house a door opens,
   closes goodbye.
The atmosphere won't
   be the same because

COMPANY (*sung after lines*): because

Baby's running from
   Mama.
Baby is a runaway.

    Mama
    runaway

Tomorrow will be a dif-
  ferent world
Than the way it was
  today.   Way it was today.
Out on the New Jersey
  Turnpike road
A hitchhiker lifts a card-   because
  board sign.
In magic marker it says   trouble
  "Anywhere"   runaway
But where I left will be
  just fine because

A prisoner's got to run
from trouble
A prisoner is a runaway.
Tomorrow will be a dif-
ferent world
Than the way it was
today.

Way it was today.

BOYS:
A man and a Lincoln
Continental,
A lawyer with a wife and
kids,

MELINDA:
Takes a plane to Reno,
doesn't turn around,

BOYS:
And doesn't care what
he did because

because

A daddy's got to run
from Mama.

Mama

A daddy is a runaway.

runaway

Tomorrow will be a dif-
ferent world
Than the way it was
today.

Way it was today.

LIDIA:
A woman gets a job in
New York City,

COMPANY:
Got to get away, got to
get away now.

LIDIA:
Forgets she was a
mother and a wife.
Got to get away, got to
get away now.

MELINDA:
Finds herself a nice
  apartment,

LIDIA AND MELINDA:
And makes up for the
  last thirty-five years
  of her life,   of her life
Because
A mama's got to run
  from Daddy.
A mama's got to run
  from child.
Tomorrow will be a dif-
  ferent world,
Lonelier and wild.

COMPANY:
Ah, ah -ey, ey
Ah, ah -ey, ey
Ah, ah -ey, ey
Ah, ah -ey, ey

MELINDA:
Thousands of cars go
  buzzing to and fro,
Airplanes and trains go
  shooting by.
Everybody goes from A
  to B,
And nobody does know
  why, because   because
The world is full of
  people running,   running
The world is made of
  runaways.   runaways
Tomorrow you'll be a
  different child
Than the one you are
  today.

Tra Gog Vo in Dein Whole
(I Will Not Tell A Soul)

Hubbell and Lazar begin a perverse, secret, sacred game: a ritual for killing off imaginary relatives in great disasters. They have their own language and their own gestures; they are making their own fabulous inner movie. They love grief and giggle at destruction.

COMPANY:
Tra gog vo in dein whole.
I will not tell a soul.
Tra gog vo in dein whole.
I will not tell a soul.
Tra gog vo in dein whole.
I will not tell a soul.

Hubbell and Lazar bring a toybox to a platform downstage, and Lidia places a toy skyscraper model in center of platform. Hubbell kneels to right of skyscraper on platform, Lazar kneels to left. Lazar removes two safari hats from the box and they are put on with great ceremony and energy.

LAZAR AND HUBBELL (*signed*):
Tra gog vo in dein whole.
I make a solemn vow.
I will not tell a soul!

The two boys salute each other. Lazar brings a doll out of the box.

LAZAR AND HUBBELL (*signed*):
Father.

Father doll is placed on tower and knocked off with rotor of toy helicopter. Hubbell pops three balloons filled with talcum powder. Both take off hats and embrace and mock crying.

LAZAR:
I'm so sorry.

Lazar cuts off crying with his hand, hats are put back on heads, Lazar takes another doll from box.

LAZAR AND HUBBELL (*signed*):
Mother.

Mother doll is placed on platform and Lazar runs her off platform with toy fire engine. Hubbell pops two more balloons, they take off hats, embrace, cry.

HUBBELL (*spoken*):
I'm so sorry.

LAZAR:
I'm sorry too.

They stop crying as before, hats are replaced, another doll taken from box.

LAZAR AND HUBBELL (*signed*):
Older brother.

Older brother doll placed on tower, another doll taken from box.

LAZAR AND HUBBELL (*signed*):
Younger sister.

Younger sister doll placed on tower, last doll taken from box.

LAZAR AND HUBBELL (*signed*):
Grandma.

Grandma doll placed on top of tower, robot taken from box.

LAZAR:
Mmmm. Elevating from box. Prepare for sibling de-
struction.
I eagerly await your orders.
Hands robot to Hubbell.
Another robot taken from box.

LAZAR:
Mmmm. Elevating from box. Prepare for filial liquidation.

Lazar and Hubbell position firing arms of robots, while making "robot" noises, and raise robots to younger sister and older brother dolls.

LAZAR AND HUBBELL (*spoken*):
Mmm, dip, dip. Mmm, dip, dip. Raga, raga, raga, raga . . . etc.

LAZAR:
Ready. (*Hubbell nods.*) Aim. (*Hubbell nods.*) Fire!

Younger sister and older brother dolls are knocked off tower. Grandma doll is shot and Lazar gives her a push off the tower with the robot and says: "Grandma!" The boys push the robots together and mimic "robot" crying.

LAZAR AND HUBBELL (*spoken in robot talk*):
I'm so sorry.

The two boys resume crying as "real" people; they embrace. Then the two boys stand, salute, jump off platform, and push platform upstage.

Revenge Song

Everyone poses for an imaginary high-school gradua-
tion photo, pretending to be "good." Revenge kindles
their spirits. They sing of their collective dream to be
famous Runaways and dance a Runaways theme song.
They are making fun of themselves.

A.J., MELINDA, ERIC:
All those days,
I was dreaming in my room for revenge.
Do you how many times
I've killed off my mother and father,
In car accidents, tragic plane crashes and with strange
   diseases?

Add LUIS, NIKKI:
All those dreams,
And once I had my science teacher roasting on a spit,
In North Alaska.
And I chewed hard on his nose.

COMPANY:
All that revenge.
And sometimes you know,
I'd imagine myself,
Breezing on a motorcycle
In an old black leather jacket
On a Midwestern highway.
And either I would end up in L.A.
With an incredible gang of far-out friends
Or I'd smash into a billboard
And end up in the intensive-care unit
Of an Arizona hospital.
And my mother and father would weep and say

LIDIA AND LUIS:	**A.J.:**
Oh we love you	ME!
best of all,	
And we'll give you	ME!
lots of presents	
from now on.	ME!

A.J.:
Oh what revenge,
Oh what sweet revenge.
But what am I now?
A loner with a sore throat,
And a blister on my toe,
And no place to go.

COMPANY:
And I used to dream of running off.
Of running far away.
And I'd see the headlines in *The New York Daily News,*

LAZAR:
"Brilliant Scholar Missing from Grieving Family,"
And hours of radio time would be filled with my description.

COMPANY:
And Stevie Wonder would write a song about me:
Poor little runaway,
Poor little runaway,
Why did you run away,
Why did you make your mommy so sad?
Oh come on back today.
Poor little runaway,
Poor little runaway,
Why did you run away?
Why did you make your mommy so sad?
Oh come on back today.

A.J.:
All these dreams. . . .

A.J. gets carried away doing his Elvis Presley act until Jackie comes up and hits him in the head. He swings back at her. Two older kids pull them apart and lift them up to stop the fight.

Enterprise

Deidre decides to instruct the audience in the art of survival. Nikki and Mex-Mongo assist her, very Supremes-style, while Deidre displays her shoplifting victories: cheese, steak, a bicycle wheel, a TV set. By the end of the song, all the Runaways are onstage with their own trophies, including a refrigerator, a hair-dryer, and a Christmas tree. They're doing a down-home looters dance after a blackout or a riot. And they're very cheerful.

DEIDRE:
One, two, three, four, five, six, seven, eight.
Here are some of the ways we survive.
There's always shoplifting at the A & P,
Pay for a pack of gum and steal a steak.
Or if security is too close by,
Eat the cheese right there.

DEIDRE, NIKKI, MEX-MONGO:
I say enterprise, you got to enterprise,
Enterprise, you got to enterprise.
And God bless the blackout when it comes.

DEIDRE:
Bicycle stealing used to be good 'til the syndicate got in on it.
But you can now and then grab a ten-speed, and sell the parts separately.
Remove the motor from a moped, or the eight-track from a car.

DEIDRE, NIKKI, MEX-MONGO:
Enterprise, you got to enterprise . . .

DEIDRE:
I go into the zoo after closing hours, and collect all the

shit from the animal cages,
Then I package it in brown paper wrappings,
And sell it as fertilizer.

DEIDRE, NIKKI, MEX-MONGO:
Enterprise, you got to enterprise . . .

DEIDRE:
I collect money for charities, orphanages or for what-

ever else I make up.
I get myself a milk container,
Wrap it in white paper,
And every day I change the name of the needy orga-
nization for which I am so unselfishly sacrificing
my time.
For instance Saint Mary's Mountain Orphanage,
The Police Athletic League,
The Little League Girls Division,
Hot Lunches for Cold Children,
Restore City Hall Incorporated,
And millions of other organizations including
project Hope, Need, Wish and Dream.

NIKKI:
Care

DEIDRE, NIKKI, MEX-MONGO:
Enterprise, you got to enterprise . . .

DEIDRE:
There's always hooking,
There's always men.
But I want to stay dignified and not do that again.

DEIDRE, NIKKI, MEX-MONGO:
Enterprise, you got to enterprise . . .

DEIDRE:
I protect helpless old ladies from potentially brutal
Muggings by my best friends here who can look like
Killers if they want to,
That's good for a quarter, a potato.

Surviving is nothing if you don't do it with imagination.
Just to get by is a waste of time.
If you want to live, you got to con.
What am I supposed to get by on?

DEIDRE, NIKKI, MEX-MONGO:
Enterprise, you got to enterprise,
Enterprise, you got to enterprise,
And God bless the blackout when it comes.

COMPANY:
YEAH!

Sometimes

Lazar is greedy. He sits down by the Christmas tree, puts his head under the hairdryer, turns on the TV, picks up a mirror, and begins to make up his face. Iggy tries to change the channel; Lazar slaps his hand. Roby and Luis warn Lazar that he's indulging himself, but he just talks back. He continues to make himself up until he looks like a grotesque rock star in horned-rim glasses.

ROBY AND LUIS:
Sometimes
too much of something is
   just as bad
as not enough
and then the pain is just
   like hunger,
strange as it seems.

COMPANY:
Sometimes

a person gets his dream
   in a big way
TV, a job, a house or a
   lover

and still he's less than
   satisfied
strange as that seems.

Sometimes
too much talking puts
   you to sleep
too much praise makes
   you feel terrible

LAZAR
(*simultaneously—
alternates with singing
lines*):

Are you going to start
   preaching at me now?
I'm still waiting for the
   little tiny ways.
I'd settle for being on the
   TV screen. Thank
   you.
I can't get no satisfac-
   tion.
It does seem just a little
   bit strange to this
   person.
Not all the time, I hope.
I am getting drowsy.

That's a problem I do not
   have, I am happy to
   say.

too much money makes
you feel cheap

strange as that seems.

ROBY AND LUIS:
Sometimes
a person gets her love in
a big way
a house, a car, maybe
some children

COMPANY:
the more she gets the
more she feels
alone and strange.

You don't want to feel
cheap?
Give me your money and
you won't feel so
cheap.
It does seem just a little
bit strange to this poor
soul.

Clothes

*Lazar's fun is interrupted when Iggy goes into a kind
of trance and tells another strange story from his past.
Lazar just stands and watches him.*

IGGY:
My mother's dead. I don't know what of. But she's
dead. And my father, who bossed her around, drank all
the time and had other girlfriends, cried a lot and said
that life was cruel. And that was it. The other night
after my mother's funeral, I went into her dresser
drawers and started sorting through her underwear, her
socks and her blouses. I could smell her powder, her
skin and her breath. I felt like number one in the world.
I mean, she got herself into one of those strange
coffins, got lowered into the ground and was never,
ever, ever seen on the face of the earth again. It was all
so mysterious, and it gave me a kind of medal to show
off. Teachers would be kinder. My friends wouldn't
say I was bad in sports and I didn't have to worry about
pimples, but then it began to wear off, and I'd hold up
the clothes and there'd be no body inside of them, and
I kept seeing the shape of her arms or the way she'd
paint her toenails. And my brain would start screaming. I mean how can a person just completely dis-
appear? I don't understand it.

Lazar crosses out Iggy's face with a black grease stick.

We Are Not Strangers II

Lazar decides to assuage Iggy's grief with drugs and booze. The Runaways light a hobo fire in a trash can and smoke reefers; they sing together. Iggy breaks an empty liquor bottle over a trash can and holds the broken bottle defiantly in the air. He teaches the youngest member of the company to do the same. It's a sort of Runaways Voodoo Reggae Ritual.

SHEILA AND EZ:
Music makes my heart sing . . . (*ad lib during rest of number*)

COMPANY:
Blow thin wind across the pines.
We have a fire to warm cold hands.
Dusty boots now rest a while.

We are not strangers.
We are not strangers.
We are not strangers.
In fact I know you well.

Have you seen the traveler's eyes?
He walked the city's streets alone.
Waited early for the sun to rise.

We are not strangers.
We are not strangers.
We are not strangers.
In fact I know you well.

Venus sits at the edge of the sky.
Don't get caught in the jails of the world.
I see how straight that black crow flies.

We are not strangers.
We are not strangers.
We are not strangers.
In fact I know you well.

The Runaways exit as sirens start to wail.

Mr. Graffiti

Mex-Mongo, a creature of the night, makes a screech-ing entrance. He shadow-boxes down the stage, ad libbing the shouts and curses of a street fight. The sides of a graffiti wall slam together behind him. (They sound just as much like a prison gate.) He turns to the audience to talk about his *way of survival—and his version of art.*

MEX-MONGO:
What is an artiste?
I don't know.
Write me a letter, Mr. Picasso.
Tell me about your spray paints and your subway wall.
What do you dream, Mr. Chagall?
I like dirty words.
I think they look right.
I paint multicolored curses late at night.
I make backgrounds of the city,
In the summer or the snow.
Is that what you did, Mr. Van Gogh?

I'd like to paint a sneaker
A hell of a sneaker
A big-ass sneaker
Big as the D train
And some day, you know
They will build
The Sneaker Subway Memorial Museum
For all of us veterans
Of Police and Graffiti wars.

For all those whose feets got electrofied
In the tracks
And for other crazy types
Who got themselves
Whammied to death
Because the train started
Itself up too soon
Just when we was in the middle
Of the most colorful and precise
Fuck You!

Have you ever met
The sixteen-year-old
Headless ghost of the 42nd Street and Broadway sub-
    way stop?
Well, I knew him when he had his head
And I saw him when he lost it.

But I like danger and nothing stops me

Would anything stop you, Mr. Salvador Dali?
(You and your signified monkey mustache!)

I sleep the whole day through
And stay awake all night
Covering the city with colors loud and bright
Under the ground
Behind the walls
Outside the windows
Like an incredible, huge, artistic, glorified, graffitified
   cockroach.

And when the stores are closed
I crawl in
And steal my spray-paint cans
Is that what you did, Masser Gauguin? Yesser, Masser.
   Yesser, Masser.

I'm serious about my art
Everybody know me
I paint my signature
All over the place
For my neighborhood to see
(This is my Mysterioso La Guardia George Washington
   Hancock Rodriguez Scooter Bozo Smith, the
   Third—Yeah!)

But what does an artiste really do
How does he live
I don't know
I can't read
But write me a letter
Mr. Preecasso Mr. Pocasso Yomamo Yopapo Yo Ugly
   Grandma, etc.

*Mex-Mongo sprays everything in sight with silly string
or spray paint.*

The Untrue Pigeon

Nikki comes down off a rooftop holding and stroking her favorite pigeon friend, Peaches. She gets lost in her romantic fairytale game with the bird.

NIKKI:
Ooo, ooo, ooo. Caw, caw, caw. Brrraaw. Brraaw. Ooo, ooo.

Well, you know, they call me the bird lady.

And I'm supposed to be one of those crazy types that talks to pigeons and pheasants and what not.

But, the truth is, that they talk to me.

And this one says to me, he says: "Hey Nikki Kay Kane, you know, I was a frog before I was a pigeon, and a prince before that, and if you would just lay your

lips on an appropriate part of my feathers, then I'm
going to take you away from all this on my big, white,
frog, pheasant, prince, horse.
Yeah!"
All right, are you ready? OK, here we go. (*kiss*) Hey!
You weren't ready, were you? One more time, ok?
Here we go. (*kiss*)
Shit.
I've got me a defective fairytale.
Hollywood's done gone and bought it all up.
You sellin' out now, huh?
And won't do nothin' for free.
Well, that's all right.
I'll just keep on talkin', and I'll keep on truckin'.
And I'll keep on ooo, ooo, ooo.
I mean, ain't there no such thing as a simple love
   between a girl and her pigeon any more?

NIKKI WITH LIDIA:
Oh, the light is coming,
Coming in the morning.
Ooo birds sing,
Ooo birds bring,
Messages so urgent.
Go, cries the bird.
Go, cries the bird.
Listen to the lovers.
Listen to the broken-hearted.
Quickly, cries the bird.
Quickly, cries the bird.

COMPANY:
Why did you leave me here alone?
Why isn't love the way it's shown in the movies?
Who will comfort me?

NIKKI WITH LIDIA:
Ooo cries the bird.
Ooo cries the bird.
Ooo.
Ooo.
Ooo.

Señoras de la Noche

Manny climbs over the tall back fence. He wears a ski mask and is a frightening vision. His eyes are on Nikki. He stalks her, grabs her, and rapes her in a dancelike motion. Then he stabs her and throws her through a window frame, which is held on either side by two Runaways who stand with their backs to the audience. Throughout, Lidia is singing her gentle song about ladies of the night. The other Runaways watch from the fences—as they watch each other die every day.

LIDIA:
Señoras de la noche
Son como luciérnagas

Tan bravas y brillantes, en la noche
Tan pálidas de día
No son mi fuego

MANNY:
Pssst.
NIKKI:
HELP!

MANNY:
(*screams*)

We Have to Die?

Nikki is on the ground, Deidre leaning over her body. Deidre is grieving to see a friend killed, but her first instinct is like an animal's—to survive. She searches Nikki's pockets, finds a few dollars, and puts them in her shirt. It's a kind of gift from Nikki. Deidre kisses Nikki's eyes.

DEIDRE:
It's bad enough we had to run away.
It's bad enough we have to safety-pin our socks to our knees and our shirts to our pants.
And walk the streets with no soles on our shoes.
That we have to live where there's no heat.
It's bad enough that we have to remember our parents' faces,
And wonder did we do wrong?
It's bad enough we gotta steal to eat,
And join disgusting gangs to feel safe.
It's bad enough that we may never see our parents again,
And if we do,

It'll be when they come to bail us out of jail,
Pick us up from the emergency room,
Or pull us from our pimps.
It's bad enough that we have to grow up having no idea
    absolutely how to talk right,
Walk cool,
Or think straight.
It's bad enough that we have to feel ashamed of what
    we can't remember,
Humiliated by what we couldn't possibly know,
And lonely for who we never met.
It's bad enough that we had to run away in the first
    place.
But we have to die too?
We have to die too?
We have to die?

*Lazar crosses out Deidre and Nikki's faces with white
grease stick.*

Where Are Those People Who Did *Hair*?

Lazar suddenly becomes a raging punk. He and Deidre join forces to mock all the "stars" of the last ten years who promised a new world with happy endings. The group joins in a tribal dance that grows wilder and wilder.

LAZAR:
Give me a *P*!

COMPANY:
P!

LAZAR:
Give me a *U*!

COMPANY:
U!

LAZAR:
Give me a *N*!

COMPANY:
N!

LAZAR:
Give me a *K*!

COMPANY:
K!

LAZAR:
What do you got?

COMPANY:
PUNK!

LAZAR:
What do you got?

COMPANY:
PUNK!

LAZAR:
What do you got?

COMPANY:
PUNK!

Music starts.

LAZAR:
I am the child of an aging hippie,
And I hate long hair like the plague. **COMPANY:**
I hate drugs because my parents are so Wooo!
  spacey.
I hate rock and roll, I say:

DEIDRE: **COMPANY:**
Any punk can play! Oooo!

LAZAR AND DEIDRE:
Where are those people who did *Hair*?
Why are they so freaky, rich and ugly?
Where are the people from San Francisco?
They got fat.

DEIDRE:
They got fat.

LAZAR AND DEIDRE:
And they bake heavy, soggy bread.
Where is the promise of a magical age?
Why do astrologists eat vegetables and fart funny?

DEIDRE:
And fart funny?

LAZAR AND DEIDRE:
Why are horoscopes computerized and tape-recorded?

DEIDRE:
Tape-recorded?

LAZAR AND DEIDRE:
Why do drugs make us furious and not peaceful like
  they said?
Like they said?

Why are half the people from rock groups in mental
   institutions?
And Kennedy and Janis Joplin and Jimi Hendrix dead.

DEIDRE:
If they were so special?

LAZAR AND DEIDRE:
Why does freedom make us empty and scared and
   belligerent,
Instead of harmonious and understanding like they
   said?
Where are those people who did *Hair*?

COMPANY:
Where are those people who did *Hair*?

LAZAR AND DEIDRE: **COMPANY:**
They're a corporation big as IBM   THINK!
and they subsidize lost and phony visions.
Where are those people who did *Hair*?

COMPANY:
Where are those people who did *Hair*?

LAZAR AND DEIDRE:
Hippies making xerox copies of the
   Beatles and smoke pot.

COMPANY:
She loves you, yeahyeahyeah

DEIDRE:
And smoke pot.

LAZAR AND DEIDRE:
McDonald's offers three free weeks of est with a fish
   cake.

COMPANY:
We do it all for you.

DEIDRE:
A fish cake.

LAZAR AND DEIDRE:
Empty happiness is turned into stupidness.
There's so much bullshit going on that by the time
   I finish this song I'll either murder someone or have
   my own special on TV!

COMPANY:
Did you know it's so easy to be a star.

LAZAR AND DEIDRE:
Where are those people who did *Hair*?

COMPANY:
Let the sun shine in. . . .

LAZAR AND DEIDRE:
Well-intentioned people who couldn't finish it.
Like social workers, organizers, presidents or priests.

COMPANY:
AMEN!

LAZAR AND DEIDRE:	**COMPANY:**
Revolution on Broadway,	HUH!
A bunch of rich naked people like me.	WOO!
Making more miserable babies like me.	WAA!
To fill up more institutions like me.	BOO!
To overdose on wasted life like me.	AGH!

COMPANY:
There's so much bullshit going on that by the time they
   finish this song they'll either murder someone or
   have their own special on TV!
Did you know . . .

LAZAR AND DEIDRE:
It's so easy to be a star.

COMPANY:
Where are those people wo did *Hair*? Let the sun
   shine in. . . .

LAZAR AND DEIDRE:	**COMPANY:**
What can they teach us from the last ten years?	HAH!
What have they done with their millions?	
They've spent a lot on Yoga, Freud and Zen,	om . . .

COMPANY:
And they saved enough, yea they saved enough,
They saved enough, yea they saved enough,
They saved enough, yea they . . . six, seven, eight,
   nine, ten

To revive *Hair* again. This is the dawning of the age
of . . .

LAZAR AND DEIDRE:
P P Do you like that?

COMPANY:
P P Do you like that?

LAZAR AND DEIDRE:
P P I'll give you more of it.

COMPANY:
P P I'll give you more of it.

LAZAR AND DEIDRE:
I don't care. I don't care.
I'll say P P to the hippies who did *Hair*.
And I sing: Death, death, death I'm getting famous.

COMPANY:
Death, death, death,

LAZAR AND DEIDRE:
I'm getting famous.

COMPANY:
Death, death, death,

LAZAR AND DEIDRE:
I'm getting closer.

COMPANY:
Death, death, death,

LAZAR AND DEIDRE:
I'm getting famous.

COMPANY:
I don't care.
I don't care.
I don't care.
To the hippies who did *Hair*. Wooooo!

Appendectomy II

While Melinda sings "Rockabye Baby" in Spanish, Jackie brings on her doll and gives it a lecture, which is also meant for herself.

MELINDA (*sung once prior to Jackie's speech, then repeated throughout*):
Duermete niño, duermete yá
Mientras tu cuna meciendiose está
Esta canción buen sueño traerá
Duermete niño, duermete yá.

JACKIE:
How sad you are, Jane. We think you must be dead.
All those appendecitises and talking-tos we gave you,
And still all you ever do is cry: "Mommy, Mommy."
How stubborn you are, Jane-Louise.
We think you must be dead.
It's too bad about all this.
You could have come and lived with us in our father's mansion in California.
And now you can't go and we can't go,
And we all have to stay here and attend your stupid, solemn funeral.
How stupid and boring, Jane-Louise.
Couldn't you have become a beauty queen or something?
But instead, a black-and-blue little girl,
With a nickel bag of grass planted where your heart should be.
And now we have to bury you so your parents will never know!

Luis and Manny—two pushers—force Jackie to insert packets of grass and heroin in the doll's stomach where the appendectomy incision was made in Act I.

Let Me Be a Kid

With Sundar jumping rope on a platform about them, the Runaways resume their street games, but they are very subdued at first. They've been through a lot. Slowly they gather strength from each other, their sense of play, and the music.

MELINDA, A.J., LIDIA:
It is so hard to be
A mother when you haven't ever had a mother's love
And it breaks my heart to be
Locked into a marriage of adult responsibility.

COMPANY:
Set me free and let me play out in the playground.
Let me be just a kid out in the playground.
Set me free and let me play out in the playground.
Let me be just a kid out in the playground.
Let me be young before I get old, let me be a kid.
Just let me be young before I get old, let me be a kid.
Just let me be young that's what I am, young
Oh, let me be young that's what I am, young
Oh, let me be young that's what I am, young
Oh, let me be young that's what I am, young

A.J., LIDIA, MELINDA, EDDIE, ROBY, EZ:
It's so hard to be
On the receiving end of grownups who demand maturity,
And it breaks my heart to see
Kids who hate themselves because they're not what they're supposed to be.

COMPANY (*simultaneously*):
Ring around the rosy, a pocket full of posey,
Ashes, ashes, we all fall down.
Ring around the rosy, a pocket full of posey,
Ashes, ashes, we all fall down.

COMPANY:
Parents make up your minds do you want children.
Parents make up your minds do you want children.

A.J., LIDIA, MELINDA, EDDIE, ROBY, EZ:
Set me free and let me play out in the playground.
Let me be just a kid out in the playground.
Set me free and let me play out in the playground.
Let me be just a kid out in the playground.
Let me be young before I get old, let me be a kid.
Just let me be young before I get old, let me be a kid.

COMPANY:
You put your right hand in,
You take your right hand out,
You put your right hand in,
And you shake it all about.
You do the hokey pokey
And you turn yourself around,
And that's what it's all about,
Hokey Pokey!
You put you whole self in,
You take your whole self out,
You put your whole self in . . .

(*finish verse as above*)

COMPANY:
Let me be young before I get old, let me be a kid.
Just let me be young before I get old, let me be a kid!

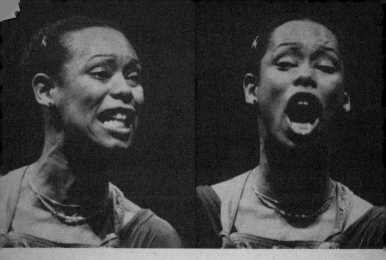

To the Dead of Family Wars

The Runways stand in a line behind Deidre with their arms around one another. As she talks her prayer, they separate one by one and start running—more frantically than before. They hum "Every Now and Then" throughout her speech.

DEIDRE:
To boys and girls whose mothers' and fathers'
Minds took long walks down late-night halls.
To boys and girls who in baby dreams,
Saw mothers and fathers scraping the strength off
    selves,
Like bark off trees.
To boys and girls whose mothers and fathers put them
    to sleep,
Not with goodnight eyes,
But goodbye.
To boys and girls who saw their mothers' and fathers'
    lives spread out,

Like caged bird wings.
To boys and girls whose mothers and fathers would
One minute give a chance,
And the next close it up like
Fat cardboard books.
To boys and girls who grew slim and adolescent
While mothers and fathers swelled with
Middle-aged wool.
When mothers and fathers stared blankly,
When mothers and fathers started screaming lines from
   old movies.
To boys and girls whose mothers and fathers drunkenly
   wished
For an incredible lie
Worth keeping.
To boys and girls who now weep,
Because you wished you'd met
Your mother's or father's shadow
On a dark talk porch,
In dream rockers.
I say,
Make laws against regret,
Otherwise, you'd have to start with Adam and Eve.
The line is long and waiting.

They were unsavable by you.
They were unseen by their own parents themselves.
It is so long this song and so yearning.
To boys and girls too young to know,
When eyes are cold and scared.
To boys and girls who in baby memories
Remember a squeeze to stop crying
So violent that it could not
Have meant
Anything but violence.
To boys and girls who in their adolescence sneak
Downstairs disturbingly found
A mother and father coiled in a chair,
Locked in consequence.
I say,
There is so much mother pull,
There is so much father pull,
And so little human decency.
To boys and girls who read half-done mother and father
   war letters,
And watch the gardens overgrow
With weeds.
To boys and girls half secret with womanhood and
   manhood,
Who have to pry open too soon,
Because mothers and fathers die or kill themselves
According to the laws of angry, random
Grownup Gods.
To boys and girls weeping, now half man, half woman
Because you wished you'd got your parents' signature,
On a definite night on a talk porch,
In dream chairs holding family hands,
Talking love words,
I say,
Make laws against regret.
Otherwise, you'd have to start with Adam and Eve,
And the line waits endlessly,
And the song is so long and so yearning.

Everyone stops running and humming.

Problem After Problem

Hubbell realizes that he can't blame anyone—but he is still full of longing. As he talks out his loneliness (he signs, his interpreter speaks), one by one the rest of the Runaways cover their faces with their shirts. They don't want photographs to be taken that could help their parents or the authorities to find them.

HUBBELL:
Problem after problem,
Mood after mood,
Sadness, despair, loneliness, anger,
I don't know how to deal with it.
No one taught me how to deal with it.
Sometimes I miss the people I left behind.
Sometimes I'm scared of the people I hang out with.
Sometimes I'm terrified I'm losing myself.
I'm telling you,
Sometimes I even think I miss my parents or something.
I want something.
I want something.
Something comforting.
Something wonderful.
Something thrilling.
Something that makes be feel!

Lonesome of the Road

The Runaways go to their hangout, the bleachers.
They sing a song of hope for each other and for anyone
else who is listening.

LUIS:
Sitting on the roof,
Watching the sun go down.

COMPANY:
Hey, people and buses and taxis you don't know what
   I'm thinking and worrying about.
But in my own way,
I'll soon find comfort,
In the lonesome of the road.

LUIS:
Out on the street,
Lonely, crazy ladies run free.

COMPANY:
I look and I'm scared and I wonder will that soon be
   me.
But in my own mind,
I'll find my reason.
In the lonesome of the road.
Take away the words, the songs, and all the things
   I had before.
Take away the city's pain and all the lies that I've
   endured.
Give me a way to survive and I'll fight for my life.
After all I'm just starting now and I've still got a while.
I've got my road map.
I've got advice from my good friends.
I've got my head clear but that's not where the struggle
   will end.
And in my own time I'll find my answers.
In the lonesome of the road.

Let Me Be a Kid (Reprise)

COMPANY:
Parents make up your minds do you want children.
Parents make up your minds do you want children.
Set me free and let me play out in the playground.
Let me be just a kid out in the playground.
Let me be young before I get old.
Let me be a kid.
Let me be young before I get old.
Let me be a kid.
Just let me be young that's what I am, young.
Oh, let me be young that's what I am, young.
Oh, let me be young that's what I am, young.
Oh, let me be young that's what I am, young.
Let me be a kid!

ELIZABETH SWADOS— A RUNAWAY TALENT

By Mel Gussow

Where do people go
when they run away?
Do they go from relative to relative
to foster home to foster home
to theater groups to therapy
to jogging to long walks
and long talks
and arguments and reconciliations?
It's all the same when you're lonely.

When she was 5 years old, a child growing up in Buffalo, Elizabeth Swados ran away from home for the first of many times. Already adept at composing songs and writing stories, she left a five-page note itemizing her grievances. Because she was afraid to cross streets by herself, her journey lasted only a few blocks and led her circuitously to an aunt's house. Soon she was safely back in her home—and contemplating another flight. All of her life—an odd expression to use about a woman who is barely 27—Liz Swados has been running from city to city, from theater group to theater group to therapy. As she asks herself, "How many times in my life have I been with adopted families?"

For years she has been a rare bird, a talented prodigal daughter. Now with her new musical, *Runaways,* opening Thursday at Joseph Papp's Public Theater Cabaret, she has become a popular creative artist. In several respects, this musical is the coming of age of Liz Swados. In it, she has also ascended to the role of "mother," or as Mr. Papp calls her, admiringly, "mother tyrant." She has led and groomed her company with a combination of maternal concern and directorial assertiveness that does not flinch from harshness when necessary. She has been a demanding schoolteacher, a patient guidance counselor and editor and a stimulant, a woman

"Elizabeth Swados—A Runaway Talent" by Mel Gussow
appeared in The New York Times Magazine, March 5, 1978.

in love with her actors and dedicated to having them operate at the very top of their potential.

Runaways, a collage of songs, monologues and scenes about children who have left home—their problems, fantasies and methods of survival—is her total creation. More than even Michael Bennett's *A Chorus Line,* which also began life as a Public Theater workshop, *Runaways* is one person's vision. It was her original idea—and she has been working on it compulsively since last May. For months, she interviewed and observed runaways; on the basis of her research, she wrote the words and music. She is the director and conductor, and she appears just offstage playing her guitar.

With the help of assistants, and the Public Theater, she coordinated the casting, choosing 19 young people between the ages of 11 and 25 from the 2,000 she interviewed. Drawn from schools, community centers and social agencies, the cast represents a broad cross section of New York. Some are actual runaways, many come from broken homes, all of them are real kids as opposed to glossy professionals. For some of them, most of their theatrical training has come under the guidance of Miss Swados. With *Runaways,* not only has she created a musical, she has also invented a company of actors. By any measure, this is a phenomenal feat, but one that seems entirely natural for this most original theatrical composer.

Her elfin face framed by a cascading curtain of long brown hair, dressed in pajamalike pantaloons, or hip boots, and a homespun jacket, and toting a book bag, she is the ultimate in contemporary casual, the personification of what once were called flower children. She looks like a waif—slender, wide-eyed and vulnerable. But she is no untutored, lost street kid. She is a highly self-disciplined, strongly motivated artist.

She comes from a family of writers, musicians and singers, which traces its roots back to Vilna, Lithuania—the family name originally was Swiadisch. Her maternal grandfather, a concert-master and violinist in Russia, emigrated to America and, unable to find employment in this profession, opened a radio and electronics store in Buffalo. Her paternal grandmother had two distinctions: She was a concert pianist and she had a lobotomy, a sequence that Miss Swados thinks of as characteristic of her "eccentric" family.

"They were strong, giddy Jewish people, very huggy-kissy," she said recently, "an extraordinarily loving, passionate brood, moody and dramatic. You had to be careful." Her mother had been an actress and a poet. Her father, Robert O. Swados, briefly considered being an actor. Now a prominent attorney in Buffalo, he is vice president and general counsel of the Buffalo Sabres hockey team and president of the board of trustees of Buffalo's Studio Arena Theater. The late, highly regarded novelist Harvey Swados was a second cousin. But the relative who was perhaps the biggest influence on her life is her "zany, mysterious" uncle Edward Maisel, a writer, world-traveler (at present he is in Java), an expert on Tai Chi and the Alexander Technique of body movement for actors and dancers.

Looking back on her childhood, Miss Swados remembers herself as a solitary individual leading an independent life. "I did things other kids didn't do," she said. She played the piano at 5, the guitar at 10, and by 12 she was performing as a folk singer (her idol was Joan Baez). As a teen-ager she wrote short stories, amassing a pile of rejection slips from *The New Yorker.* She recalls occasional collisions with her parents, usually over her extravagant disorder: Once she filled a room "waist deep" with paper cutouts of people, gas stations, hospitals. Often in collaboration with her brother (he is eight years older and lives in New York), she created private worlds of the imagination.

The Swados household was filled with animals, dogs, ducks, parakeets. About her pets, she said, "Some died, some were given away, some ran away." As for Liz, "I was rebellious, but with one eye open." Her own runaways were planned, extended excursions.

At 16, she left Buffalo to go to Bennington College and never again lived in her childhood home. At Bennington, she studied music and creative writing and was something of a "black sheep" in the music department. Her "first symphony" was a symphonic overture in which 30 actors posed as a Balinese monkey chorus. Her other primary mark of distinction at college was having her photograph in *The New York Times Magazine* in 1969 as "the first woman at Bennington to celebrate its new-found coeducation by moving in with one of the six new men."

Periodically she left Bennington, on work programs and summer projects. For two summers she sang and played the guitar with Pete Seeger on his sloop, the *Clearwater.* During her second term, she moved from Bennington to West Virginia, where she lived with an Appalachian family, tutored children, taught theater, started a newspaper and made a public protest against black-lung disease. In a short period of time, she seemed to try everything: commune life, vegetarianism and drugs. "I did everything," she says, "with the passion of thinking, what's going to become of me?"

While still a student at Bennington, she began working at Ellen Stewart's Café La Mama in New York. The indomitable Miss Stewart is truly La Mama, the mother of Off Off Broadway, and Miss Swados became one of her many creative children. At La Mama, Miss Swados worked with a number of foreign directors, most significantly with Andrei Serban. Serban, about to embark on his innovative version of *Medea,* enlisted Miss Swados to write the eerily authentic score. Miss Swados's score demonstrated her ability to be what she calls a musical "chameleon." Having left Bennington before graduation, she submitted her *Medea* score as a sign of her work and received her degree in absentia. The team of Serban and Swados, with their company as family, triumphantly toured Europe and the Middle East, performing their adaptations of *Electra* and *The Trojan Women* as well as *Medea.*

During her association with Serban, Miss Swados spent a year working with Peter Brook's troupe, traveling through Africa with guitar and tape recorder, preparing the performance piece "The Conference of the Birds." The troupe would stop in tiny villages and try to communicate with natives, using stories and songs. Africa brought her closer to animals; birdcalls became her musical trademark.

Some of her memories of Brook's company are carved into her skin. Between the thumb and forefinger of her right hand she has a tattoo, two intertwined halves of triangles. It is an Aztec sign that means, "You are my other self. If I love and protect you, I love and protect myself. If I do harm to you, I do harm to myself." Miss Swados recalls, "I got incredibly drunk with an American Indian actor and we had a tattooing orgy. I don't regret it. But I don't have to have the tattoo on my hand to be moved by the message."

On her leg is another tattoo, a checkerboard calligraphy that is a Japanese sign for good life—"like *mazel tov.*" And then, a little shyly, she admits that she has a third tatoo, a triangle on her left shoulder. "When I was in Africa, I had malaria," she said. "Every time I looked up at the sky, I would see a triangle." A touch of mysticism to add to her quest for identity? Was she also trying to hurt herself? "A lot of kids in run-away homes cut themselves with knives," she answered. No matter how bizarre her behavior, nothing interfered with her work. "I could be carving myself up and getting tattoos," she said, "but if a song is due, I'm going to finish it."

Almost four years ago, while in Brazil with Serban discussing a production of *The Trojan Women*, came the most traumatic moment of Miss Swados's life. She received word from Buffalo that her mother had committed suicide. She immediately flew back to be with her family. "What an unusually spiteful, horrendous act!" she said about her mother's suicide. "A parent leaving a legacy that life is no good, that the solution to problems is to die. The world began to look like that parent. I was mad at everybody—Ellen, Andrei, Peter, everybody"—all of her substitute parents.

Trying to understand her mother's act, she said, "I think she was frustrated. She wanted to be more than a housewife in Buffalo. When she was depressed, she tried everything—meditation, yoga, exercise," and nothing seemed to work. "I do believe it shouldn't have happened." Miss Swados's gloom was deepened by the death, within a year and a half's time, of three of her mother's sisters. "Such a shock," she said. "Everyone conked out." Her family decimated, she felt even more adrift. "I was a wreck," she said, "but I did not fall apart." She went into therapy. "I learned to be sad, to feel gypped and afraid, and then to say, enough of that, to channel it, to regain faith in people."

Contemplating her family's tragedies and eccentricities, she said, "A family's history has an enormous effect on an individual. Those demons certainly exist in me. There is pain. But the lucky thing is that they are a great help, a source of enormous energy and perception. They're partially responsible for my creative energy, my need to write music. I strongly believe that unless there are chemical imbalances—which I don't have—the individual can determine whether he succumbs or not. People in my family have gone both ways—off the deep end, or, like my father, using his energy to accomplish things, to be productive, and giving. It's a fight. It's probably made me stronger than most people who come from sedate families. Let me say that my family had incredible humor. My mother had one of the greatest senses of humor. I'm not an unhappy person. I live in wild swings of mood but I sure live!"

Even in her depression, she worked—and found salvation

in work. For Serban, she wrote scores of remarkable diversity—more than 60 songs for their spirited version of *The Good Woman of Setzuan* and moody background scores for *The Cherry Orchard* and *Agamemnon* at Lincoln Center.

Up to this point, her theatrical work had been in collaboration with others—and only as a composer. The scores reflected the serious side of her nature, but there was another, younger, fun-loving and self-satiric Swados. By her own admission, she has a penchant for being "a joker, a clown, a trickster," even a con artist. Suitably, the first theater piece created entirely by herself was *Nightclub Cantata,* an exuberant theatrical vaudeville. *Cantata,* an overt attempt to let her long hair down, was an eclectic revue, a pastiche of songs, dances and sketches, which celebrated various writers (Delmore Schwartz, Pablo Neruda, Sylvia Plath) as well as the art of entertainment. A highlight was the pseudo-death-defying circus adventures of the "legendary" Pastrami Brothers (after a loud fanfare, one brother touches another's arm with his index finger). *Cantata,* written and directed by Miss Swados and featuring her in the original cast, playing the guitar and trilling and cooing like a bird, was a hit Off Broadway last season and also sent companies to Boston, Washington and Europe.

About the time that *Cantata* was conceived, she also had the idea for *Runaways.* The success of the former won her many offers—for movies as well as musicals. Rejecting commercial sponsorship of her runaway idea, she elected to work under the auspices of Mr. Papp, who promised her the cherished commodities of time and freedom.

The idea for *Runaways* did not come from contemplating ghetto children, but from her own life and her feeling of "fragmentation." Looking back on her experiences with Brook and Serban, she said, "Every time I thought I was putting on a play, I ended up with a family. It always has to do with family—the most interesting repeated message of my semiadult existence. I wanted to see if I could translate that into a musical metaphor. The show uses young runaways as a metaphor for leaving home. It doesn't say it's good to have a family. It shows what happens when people don't have a family—as a point of identity or as a place to be. It can lead to danger, exploitation and abuse—or to something beautiful. I'm not by any stretch of the imagination a ghetto kid or an abused child, but I can strongly relate to the metaphor."

Two other reasons encouraged her interest. "I look at people like musical instruments. I set people to music. Adolescence is an extraordinary age; the audacity is something. They try every drug—in dreams and in action. The most intense feelings, desires, imaginations! That energy is tremendous. These kids are like a raw piece of music and you can orchestrate it. I don't see them as adorable kids." She continued, "The *really* important reason I'm doing this is that I *love* popular music: soul, salsa, jazz, country-western. I can't believe myself doing it. If I write a pop song, because of my intellectual literary background, I tend to think I'm slipping. People I've worked with don't really believe that music. But pop music moves me as much as Delmore Schwartz does. I wanted to do this before I intellectualized myself into oblivion. I thought, there's still a chance for you, Swados. Two-chord rock songs and lyrics that rhyme instead of Sylvia Plath. The artist in me should tremble. Instead, she's giggling like hell."

For research, she read, among other books, *Weeping in the Playtime of Others* by Kenneth Wooden, "a passionate document of truth" about abused children and Tom Wicker's book about Attica, *A Time to Die*. Last June she began a firsthand study, acting as both investigative reporter and folklorist, interviewing adolescents and even hanging around schoolyards, amassing material—anecdotes, catch phrases, dreams, methods of survival, street poetry.

At the same time, she began looking for possible members of her new company. Since her plan was to have the cast work half-time on the project for five months—school in the morning, rehearsal in the afternoon—she needed permission from schools. As an inducement, she used Mr. Papp's name and his clout when necessary. In only one instance did a school deny permission. To her chagrin, that was the High School of Performing Arts—and she had high hopes for her chosen candidate. "We got kids out of P. S. 125 and Hunter, but Performing Arts wouldn't let us. Why not? So that the girl could go to Juilliard after finishing high school and then try to be in a show like ours? To me, theater is an apprentice job. You don't go to school for it. You have to do it."

She avoided professional schools and turned instead to storefront cultural centers, the Theater of the Forgotten and The Door, a Lower East Side center for alternative studies. Discussing her criteria for selection, she said, "The main thing is I had to like them. Also I looked for imagination, coordination and feistiness. They're all feisty as hell. They're just people, not stars; they have a gift for being themselves. Intelligence, warmth and a certain ability to understand political concepts, but I didn't want a psychologist in my company,'' although her pianist, Judith Fleisher, is also a psychologist. What about talent? ''Absolutely, but not conventional theatrical talent. Every kid who made it was called back six or seven times. Partly it was a matter of endurance. How much did they want it? This is not a good-will program. I can't accept everybody.''

Typical of the children whom she chose is Anthony Imperato. He is 14 and he is short. He looks like a tough, handsome street kid, the kind who might grow up and become James Cagney. He has absolutely no professional experience, but he has a natural flair for performing and he has always wanted to be an actor. Recalling Miss Swados's unusual audition, he said, ''We did movements, passed around the basketball and made noises. My Dad said, 'Don't get your hopes too high,' I said, 'Dad, I *want* to make it. I want to be something. I don't want to be a guy on the street.' ''

In August, Miss Swados left New York with a friend, driving south through the Carolinas and Georgia. On the trip she filled notebooks with everything that was on her mind about runaways and running away. Because she is, first of all, a composer, the words naturally formed themselves into songs —songs about isolation and loneliness, graffiti, basketball, skateboarding, teen-age prostitution, drugs, con games. The songs and the poetic monologues drew on her research and also on incidents from her own life: a girl operating on a doll, another child fantasizing about having famous parents (''I am the undiscovered son of Judy Garland''). Writing musical notes over the words, she then sang her songs into a tape recorder.

In the fall, she began broadening and diversifying the cast. She chose one deaf child from a very close family in which everyone is deaf, and, feeling that she had been prejudiced against professionals, she chose several with experience— including three from *Cantata* companies and 13-year-old Diane Lane, who had been in Serban's Greek trilogy. In those tragedies Miss Lane had suffered horrible deaths on stage. When she was invited to be in *Runaways,* she pleaded, ''Don't make me die!'' In *Runaways,* she gets to sing and dance.

Bernard Allison, Bernie to his friends, is a skateboard

champion. With his skateboard, he has traveled to Europe and California. Tall, athletic-looking, he is a health-food faddist and something of a mystic. Written on his favorite T-shirt is the slogan, "Additives: the Perfect Crime." He was born in New York 22 years ago and was discovered at the Door, where he was about to give a workshop on skateboarding. In *Runaways* he plays "the hero"—doing a balletic dance on a skateboard.

"I needed transportation," he explains. "A skateboard is faster than walking, easier than running. I skated 200 miles to Santa Cruz. I want to skate to Washington. Skateboarding is a way of finding my center and also a medium for meeting people. I'm writing a play about skateboarding and a book about nonviolent kung fu. I'm a fruitarian; I drink juice, eat dried apricots, raw cashews.

"I ran away at 4. When I met my real mother, I ran away again. I've gone from foster home to foster home. I left high school in the first year. I just can't follow a structure. I've worked as a messenger, but I can't keep jobs like that. In 1973 I threw out all my clothes. When I got rid of things, I became more giving. I'm training for the rope-skipping record. I hate violent sports.

"Liz is an excellent director. The only thing I don't like is the yelling. I respond better to gentleness. I hope the show moves to Broadway, but whenever it ends, I'll move on to something else. I don't like big cities. I like mountains, clean air, peacefulness. I'm going to change my name, maybe to something Polynesian or something to do with nature. Sitting Bull! Rolling Thunder! My best friend is my skateboard."

David Schechter has wild hair, antic eyes and the face of a clown. At 21, he is already a vaudeville zany. A graduate of Bard College, he was one of the original Pastrami Brothers in *Nightclub Cantata* and is one of the more experienced actors in *Runaways*. His ferocious punk-rock travesty is a sure showstopper. He grew up on Grand Street in Manhattan.

"I was taken to the theater from the age of 4," he says. "My aunt was a stage-door Johnny. I listened to musical-comedy records. I was an actor from the word go. I ran away from school and was put in private school. I went to Bard when I was 16. Once I ran away from a show. We invited Liz up to Bard and I went right into *Cantata*. I did 281 performances. At the Arena Stage we stole our Pastrami Brothers costumes. Once I went to an open call—for *Pippin*.

It was horrible. When I came into this, I felt I was going to be the most experienced. But there's so much energy here. The whole age thing disappeared. I love this cast. I feel like these are some of my best friends.

"Liz wants total surrender from the actor. I can trust her now. I try to be tuned in to her every second. She makes incredible demands. She'll have someone run for five minutes while delivering a speech. I have to beat myself up in the show. It's exhausting and painful and you curse while you're doing it. But you give a lot and your body grows a lot. It's very nervous at the beginning of each day, a constant challenge. But I like to be a little over my head."

Leonard Brown, who is 20, calls himself Duke. It says "Duke" on his tank-top shirt. He corn-rolls his hair and tries to look menacing, but he is sweet and gentle and sings in a high, golden voice.

Describing his entry into the theater, he says, "There was a workshop on my block, 174th Street in the Bronx, so I checked it out. I dug it and I did plays, toured homes and prisons. I sang and learned to play the drums and piano just by playing. I quit high school. I don't like being told what to do. Music is practically my whole life—opera, ballet, disco. I went to one ballet. I always wanted a high voice, like Michael of the Jackson Five. When I was 18, the voice started coming. I worked on it. The first singing groups had me on the bottom. I always wanted to be on top. This is the first really professional thing I've been in. We work hard, but at the end of the day I'm not tired. If it was like school, I'd be bored to death. The teacher writes on the board and I fall asleep. I ran away twice—one-night stands. After I got hungry, I went home. I never had the heart to be out alone.

"The first play I saw was *Purlie,* then *Colored Girls* and *The Wiz* three times. I wouldn't mind doing *The Wiz*. If this goes to Broadway, I'll go with it. If not, I'll go to Pratt and further my acting. I'd like to deejay for a radio station. I've done messenger jobs and been a mail clerk and never really enjoyed myself. Here I can do practically everything I like—play the drums, sing, dance, play basketball. I'm learning and I'm happy."

Each actor was paid $75 a week for rehearsals as well as performances and, for some, extra money up to $25 a week was made by doing extra work—acting as assistant stage manager, tutoring, or taking care of the pigeons that became a part of the show. Once public previews began, the actors were paid Equity scale, $180 a week. "At first they just thought I was crazy and incredible," Miss Swados said, "then, that opportunity had fallen in their laps."

From the first, her approach to the actor-adolescents was extremely professional. "Ambiguity is the huge killer," she said. To encourage their diligence, she fined them for lateness, $5 for the first half-hour, $7.50 for the next 10 minutes if they did not call in. Some of the street con, practiced outside the theater, was applied in the workshop—phony excuses left at the Public Theater switchboard. Miss Swados responded by getting tougher.

She did not condone laziness or indolence in any context. Mr. Papp once heard her say to a member of the cast: "Sing it louder or you'll be replaced." That threat always hung over their heads. She publicly criticized everyone from the youngest to the oldest, even including the musicians, who are old friends and associates. At first, some of the youngsters would cry in response to criticism, but soon their skins got thicker. An effective actress, Miss Swados can escalate her anger at will. In her biggest explosion, she threw her script and all of her notes into the air. Like snowflakes, they floated around the rehearsal room, the youngsters staring in amazement.

Miss Swados can display a violent temper, triggered by dissatisfaction, usually with herself. When a composition is not going well, she has been known to slam her fist through her guitar. "I'm a great tape-recorder smasher," she said. "I buy cheap models. I throw them on the floor and stamp on them. I'm not advocating that. I hate primal therapy and things like that." Her anger is a conscious choice. "I can choose to be unstable. I have all the makings for a nervous breakdown, but I want to *do* a lot of things. I work most of the time. The way to survive is to work and to live entirely in the moment."

But with all the criticism came appreciation. Acknowledgment, even admiration, from Miss Swados was like getting an apple from the teacher. She prodded her company to perform better, edged them toward perfectionism, but along with leadership there was genuine affection. The company was a close family.

One day Miss Swados auditioned for a cast replacement. Six black actresses showed up. They had come from various sources; several had previously read for road companies of

For Colored Girls Who Have Considered Suicide/When the Rainbow is Enuf. She asked them to "make up a country and a ritual of that country and do a little song and dance to go with that ritual." Such auditions throw actors back on their resources—and some flail, resorting to packaged readings and self-conscious bits of business. A few of these actresses easily improvised, others fell into stock showmanship. Then the director went around a circle, making a different sound to each woman, saying, "Imitate me to the T. Making fun of me is O.K."

To a buxom young woman in white slacks, one not as glamorous as her peers, she said, "Ba-lo-ney! Baloney!" The woman followed her up and down the scales, spitting back each syllable of "baloney." At the end of the audition, Miss Swados conferred with an assistant. There was no doubt about her decision: The woman in white who said "baloney" was chosen for her feistiness. But, within days, the woman had been fired. She did not fit into the group, by then a tight unit. She was too aggressive. "I thought they would kill her," said Miss Swados.

Mornings, the youngsters went to their individual schools, or other occupations. Miss Swados tried to catch up on her special projects, usually working in her Greenwich Village coach-house apartment, which she shares with her dog, Mushroom, "a poodle who looks like a bear." She has been writing the music for a television documentary about Marcel Duchamp and setting Samuel Beckett poems to music.

Every afternoon, the company came together in private, Miss Swados sitting on a gym mat facing the cast and strumming her guitar—the cast, the musicians, a stage manager, a woman doing sign language for the deaf actor, and myself as frequent observer.

In its earliest stages, the group exercised—physically, vocally, emotionally and strenuously. Miss Swados has codified thousands of exercises, and she introduced them to the ensemble. For example, she would ask one to make a sound and to pass it around the circle, altering it slightly with each repetition. Each would tell stories, how they conned someone, or about a time when they were afraid. Often, Miss Swados talked about herself; she told them about her mother's suicide.

One day she brought in a carload of cardboard boxes of various sizes and shapes and asked the youngsters to label them with emotions: resignation, anger, despair, wanting, joy, peace, and then to improvise scenes in and around them. The smallest box was "help." The most unpopular box was "peace." During this session, Mr. Papp happened to walk in—and he played the game. He said that his favorites among the boxes were "wanting" and "danger," which, coincidentally, were the first choices of the company.

The group moved to a semipermanent rehearsal space in a building across from the theater. A basketball net was erected and at intervals everyone, including the director, played a mad, scrambling game—a herd of people running and shouting. Planks of wood were nailed together to create a semblance of a shelter; later, Douglas Schmidt would design a set, a representation of a playground. Soon the space began to seem like a cross between a crash pad, an attic and a schoolyard.

As I watched, over the weeks, the children grew in confidence and in ability. They even sharpened their appearance. One large young black woman gradually began to lose her excess weight, peeling away the pounds and revealing a certain statuesque beauty. Diane Lane blossomed into young womanhood. Relationships and rivalries developed. Some became best friends. There were, as Miss Swados observed, "heartbreak, humiliation and rage—people storming out and weeping in the bathroom."

The transition from workshop to full production was organic. Actors were given songs, dances, monologues. Roles were switched and expanded. Songs were dropped and new lyrics written. The show took the natural shape of the participants. For example, with the presence of Bernie Allison, a skateboard champion, in the cast, there was no doubt that there would be skateboard choreography. Tony Butler's prowess as a graffiti artist assured that he would paint "multicolored curses" during the show. One day, Jonathan Feig brought in his violin; he now plays it on stage. More and more, the director stressed enunciation, intelligibility, voice volume and concentration.

The turning point in this adventure may have been reached on a day in early December when Miss Swados took her troupe on a field trip to the Kennedy Home in the Bronx. Originally a home for retarded children, funded by the Kennedy family, over the years it has become a center for disturbed children. Many of them are dead-end runaways, filled with anger, resentment and even panic (the home was scheduled to be closed soon). As the members of the troupe entered the home, they were swept away by an immediate sense of insecurity. It was as if they were suddenly facing their life models, what they had only been pretending to be.

Addressing the residents of the home, Miss Swados asked key questions, such as "Whom do you hate?" In a chorus came the answer, "The guidance counselor!" Why? "Because he's very cool." At the director's suggestion, one youth in her company swaggered out and playacted being cool. Then on cue, another mimed smoking a reefer and another seethed with anger. There was a roar of approval from the audience. What do you do when you're angry? "Break a window!" said one resident of the home. Miss Swados encouraged the speaker to act it out, as officials of the home watched, barely containing their shudders: They thought she might really break a window. How do you survive on the street? The two groups came together and enthusiastically began comparing con games.

The immediate communication, the vocalization of shared concerns, was visceral—a one-on-one connection. The members of the ensemble were made vividly aware of the seriousness of their project, and the Kennedy children looked upon their visitors as professionals—as "actuhs." For the company it was like opening night. An intensely private workshop, a study in process, was, as intended, on its way to going public.

In mid-December the group held its first full run-through before an audience, composed of Mr. Papp; his wife, Gail Merrifield, who is the Public's director of play development; and about a dozen other friends and associates. They sat in a long, straight line of chairs facing the actors. Miss Swados jokingly referred to the terrifying afternoon as "our backer's audition." Actually, in the solemnity of the occasion, it seemed more like an appearance before a parole board. Up to then, Miss Swados says, Mr. Papp had been "powerful, lethal, but scarce; he does not hang out." To the group he was the boss; in fact, they called him "the boss."

The songs soared. Some of the kids performed with ease, others were forced. And there were awkward transitions between scenes. The director stopped one youth in midsong and charged, "You're singing like a turkey!" And he was. In the middle of one number satirizing the system ("You've got to enterprise . . ."), the stage suddenly became chaotic.

"Stop, stop!" she shouted. "Concentrate!" But when the ensemble sang the tender "Where do people go/When they run away?" the room seemed to glow with emotion.

That evening, the boss and the mother tyrant had a conference. He offered strong suggestions. Anything that reminded him of *Hair* and *A Chorus Line* should be removed. There should be more humor and more solos. The structure should be strengthened, perhaps with a character such as Diane Lane's child prostitute threading through the show. Miss Swados assented to all but the last. This was not, and would not be, a structured musical. By its very nature, it was loose, episodic and spontaneous. *Runaways* went back to workshop.

At the end of the week, I wandered by in midafternoon and the entire cast was gathered in front of a television set. They were watching their Christmas present, the best present a kid could have—*Star Wars*. Someone had obtained a tape, and they were all eagerly watching it. Any sign that these might be polished professionals vanished. They were kids on a holiday! At a certain point, the director decided to stop the movie and return to rehearsal. Revolution! One youth promised to work 15 more minutes every day for the next two weeks if she would let the movie continue. "I can't compete with *Star Wars*," resolved Miss Swados. She relented: another half-hour of the movie, then rehearsal, and if all went well, they would stop early and see the end of the movie.

The following week, she gathered the company and gave them a pep talk. "It's time. It's time. If you're an actor and you have to cough, you don't cough. If you're not enough of an actor, you leave. You're going to give seven or eight performances a week and I'm not going to be there to scream at you. This is for your own safety. It really gets dangerous out there. You have to start building up stamina. I'm going to ask for more and more. . . ."

With the show steadily improving, suddenly one of the youngsters quit the cast. He was one of the few who had been a professional before he joined the company, and his agent had gotten him a role in a movie. Matter-of-factly, he informed Miss Swados, perhaps expecting her blessing. Instead, she exploded. He had joined the company under false pretenses, wasted months of their time, abused his relationship with the other youngsters. Feeling that the boy was remorseless, and that his act was reprehensible, especially considering the time invested, she accelerated her attack until he cried. Then, tearfully, he asked if he could go to the bathroom. "It's no longer your bathroom," she said, and dismissed him from the theater. Explaining his resignation to the other actors was heartbreaking: The boy who quit had run away from the family.

As the show approached its first public performance, the boss saw it again and felt that it "was not tough enough." Working closely with Mr. Papp as artistic adviser, Miss Swados made *Runaways* angrier and sharper. The total focus was on the youngsters; the few scenes in which they had played adults were excised. The show became less specifically about ghetto kids and more about kids; in other words, it became more relevant to its author herself and to the audience.

In the monologues—harsh and poignant—the children talked about their hopes and their fantasies: smashing in the television set when parents ignore the fact that they have returned after running away, hysterical current-events recitations that record our daily horrors. With all the changes in tone, performance and texture, and the several changes in cast—a few actors were actually fired—several things remained constant: the enthusiasm—the hunger—of the actors (many of them dreamed about Broadway); Miss Swados as sympathetic mother tryant; and the music. As is usual with this composer, the score was eclectic, in this case moving from salsa to disco, samba to blues, gospel to flamenco, and including a show-stopping knockout travesty of punk rock ("Where are the people who did *Hair?*"), contemporary ballads, country-western, Brazilian and African percussion, and even a number ("Revenge") with the beat of a strip song. There is also, of course, one bird song, crooned to a New York City pigeon. The bird song is Miss Swados's signature —"my Alfred Hitchcock."

Although she makes no secret about her suspicion of some aspects of her profession, she also has great admiration for consummate professionals such as Sarah Vaughan. Whenever Miss Vaughan appears in New York, Miss Swados goes to see her, and watches in silent admiration. "She's a brilliant virtuoso," she said. "If I could do something for the human race, it would be what she does for me." She would love to hear Miss Vaughan sing "Every Now and Then" from *Runaways*—but not as an actress in the show.

She reiterated her artistic position: "A musical piece is defined by what plays it. Take a classical piece and reorchestrate it—and it changes. If this show succeeds, it's because of the kids *and* the material. These are the best possible voices for this material. Do you want to hear Joan Sutherland sing the punk-rock song? Do you want a show or a showcase for material? Barbra Streisand could sing 'I'm Sorry.' But where are the runaways? Later on, someone could say, that's a great song for Streisand. She could record it, but that's another form. I've chosen this form. When I did *Agamemnon*, intellectually I was in pain trying to make that piece work, but I didn't wake up in the morning and think about poor Iphigenia. But doing this, I wake up and worry about the listlessness of people's lives—and the loneliness."

Set me free and let me play out in the playground
And let me be just a kid out in the playground
Let me be young before I get old
Let me be a kid.

ABOUT THE AUTHOR

ELIZABETH SWADOS was born in Buffalo, New York, in 1951. She is a graduate of Bennington College. Swados started her theater career at Ellen Stewart's La Mama ETC, then worked for a year with Peter Brook's *The Conference of the Birds* in Paris, Africa and America. In collaboration with Andrei Serban, she wrote the music for the operas *Medea, Electra, The Trojan Women, Agamemnon* and *The Good Woman of Setzuan*. In 1976 she composed and directed *Nightclub Cantata,* which was produced off-Broadway with companies in Boston, Washington and Europe. At Joseph Papp's Public Theater she composed and directed *Runaways* (1978), *Alice* (based on *Alice in Wonderland,* 1979), and *Dispatches* (1979). In addition to composing numerous film scores for NBC, CBS, PBS and independent films, she wrote "Truth and Variation" for the National Ballet of Canada in 1979. Her books for children are *The Girl with the Incredible Feeling* (which she also adapted into a theater piece) and *The First Step,* with Faith Hubley, for the International Year of the Child. Swados's first orchestral work, *New York Gypsy Suite,* will be presented in the spring of 1980 at the Carnegie Recital Hall with the Orchestra of New York. Swados is currently at work on the screenplay of the 20th Century Fox film of *Runaways.*

DISCOVER
THE DRAMA OF LIFE
IN THE LIFE OF DRAMA

☐	13434	**CYRANO DE BERGERAC** Rostand	$1.75
☐	12204	**FOUR GREAT PLAYS** Ibsen	$1.95
☐	11881	**COMP. PLAYS SOPHOCLES**	$2.25
☐	11936	**FOUR GREAT PLAYS BY CHEKHOV** Anton Chekhov	$1.75
☐	13001	**THE NIGHT THOREAU SPENT IN JAIL** Jerome Lawrence and Robert E. Lee	$1.95
☐	13390	**RUNAWAYS** Elizabeth Swados	$2.50
☐	12832	**THE PRICE** Arthur Miller	$1.95
☐	13363	**BRIAN'S SONG** Blinn	$1.95
☐	12548	**THE EFFECTS OF GAMMA RAYS ON MAN-IN-THE-MOON MARIGOLDS** Paul Zindel	$1.95
☐	12711	**50 GREAT SCENES FOR STUDENT ACTORS** Lewy Oltson, ed.	$1.95
☐	12917	**INHERIT THE WIND** Lawrence & Lee	$1.75
☐	13102	**TEN PLAYS BY EURIPIDES** Hadas	$2.50
☐	12418	**THE CRUCIBLE** Arthur Miller	$1.95
☐	12214	**THE MIRACLE WORKER** Gibson	$1.75
☐	11777	**AFTER THE FALL** Arthur Miller	$1.95

Buy them at your local bookstore or use this handy coupon for ordering:

TEENAGERS FACE LIFE AND LOVE

Choose books filled with fun and adventure, discovery and disenchantment, failure and conquest, triumph and tragedy, life and love.

☐	13359	**THE LATE GREAT ME** Sandra Scoppettone	$1.95
☐	10946	**HOME BEFORE DARK** Sue Ellen Bridgers	$1.50
☐	11961	**THE GOLDEN SHORES OF HEAVEN** Katie Letcher Lyle	$1.50
☐	12501	**PARDON ME, YOU'RE STEPPING ON MY EYEBALL!** Paul Zindel	$1.95
☐	11091	**A HOUSE FOR JONNIE O.** Blossom Elfman	$1.95
☐	12025	**ONE FAT SUMMER** Robert Lipsyte	$1.75
☐	13184	**I KNOW WHY THE CAGED BIRD SINGS** Maya Angelou	$2.25
☐	13013	**ROLL OF THUNDER, HEAR MY CRY** Mildred Taylor	$1.95
☐	12741	**MY DARLING, MY HAMBURGER** Paul Zindel	$1.95
☐	12420	**THE BELL JAR** Sylvia Plath	$2.50
☐	12338	**WHERE THE RED FERN GROWS** Wilson Rawls	$1.75
☐	11829	**CONFESSIONS OF A TEENAGE BABOON** Paul Zindel	$1.95
☐	11632	**MARY WHITE** Caryl Ledner	$1.95
☐	13352	**SOMETHING FOR JOEY** Richard E. Peck	$1.95
☐	13440	**SUMMER OF MY GERMAN SOLDIER** Bette Greene	$1.95
☐	11839	**WINNING** Robin Brancato	$1.75
☐	13004	**IT'S NOT THE END OF THE WORLD** Judy Blume	$1.75

Buy them at your local bookstore or use this handy coupon for ordering:

Bantam Book Catalog

Here's your up-to-the-minute listing of over 1,400 titles by your favorite authors.

This illustrated, large format catalog gives a description of each title. For your convenience, it is divided into categories in fiction and non-fiction—gothics, science fiction, westerns, mysteries, cookbooks, mysticism and occult, biographies, history, family living, health, psychology, art.

So don't delay—take advantage of this special opportunity to increase your reading pleasure.

Just send us your name and address and 50¢ (to help defray postage and handling costs).

BANTAM BOOKS, INC.
Dept. FC, 414 East Golf Road, Des Plaines, Ill. 60016

Mr./Mrs./Miss_____
                              (please print)

Address_____

City_____State_____Zip_____

Do you know someone who enjoys books? Just give us their names and addresses and we'll send them a catalog too!

_____

Mr./Mrs./Miss_____

Address_____

City_____State_____Zip_____

_____

Mr./Mrs./Miss_____

Address_____

City_____State_____Zip_____

FC—9/78